Baking Soda

House & Home

Publisher's Note:
All reasonable care has been exercised by the author and publisher to ensure that the tips and remedies included in this guide are simple and safe. However, it is important to note that all uses of baking soda should be practised with caution and a doctor's, or relevant professional's, advice should be sought if in any doubt or before any topical or medicinal usage. Neither the editors, the author nor the publisher take responsibility for any consequences of any application which results from reading the information contained herein.

Please note also that the measurements provided in this book are presented as metric/imperial/US-cups practical equivalents, and that all eggs are medium (UK)/large (US) respectively unless otherwise stated.

This is a **FLAME TREE** book
This edition first published in 2014

Publisher and Creative Director: Nick Wells
Project Editor: Catherine Taylor
Picture Research: Katie Pimlott, Catherine Taylor, Harrison Fertig
Art Director: Mike Spender
Layout Design: Jane Ashley
Digital Design and Production: Chris Herbert

Thanks to Polly Prior, Daniela Nava, Helen Snaith

16 18 17 15

3 5 7 9 10 8 6 4

FLAME TREE PUBLISHING
6 Melbray Mews
Fulham, London SW6 3NS
United Kingdom

www.flametreepublishing.com

© 2014 this edition Flame Tree Publishing Ltd

ISBN 978-1-78361-309-0

A CIP Record for this book is available from the British Library upon request.

Printed in China

Baking Soda

House & Home

Diane Sutherland, Jon Sutherland, Liz Keevill and Kevin Eyres

FLAME TREE PUBLISHING

Contents

Introduction

If you could find a naturally occurring product that you could use as a deodorant, a toothpaste, an exfoliant and an antiseptic, you would be impressed. If you found out that you could use the same substance in the kitchen to make a big improvement to many of your favorite dishes, and then use it to clean out your pots and pans, leaving them grease-free and shining, you would be amazed. And if you were told that exactly the same product could be used to shampoo your pets, clean out your swimming pool, kill cockroaches and relieve insect bites and stings, you'd probably just laugh. Well, there is just such a product, it's been around for thousands of years in one form or another and you can buy it today for pennies.

It All Started in Ancient Egypt

When the ancient Egyptians needed something that would keep mummified bodies dry and free from bacteria on their journey through the afterlife, they found the answer: a sodium compound, occurring naturally in dry lake beds. They called the substance Natron because a particularly good source was an area called Wadi-el-Natrun.

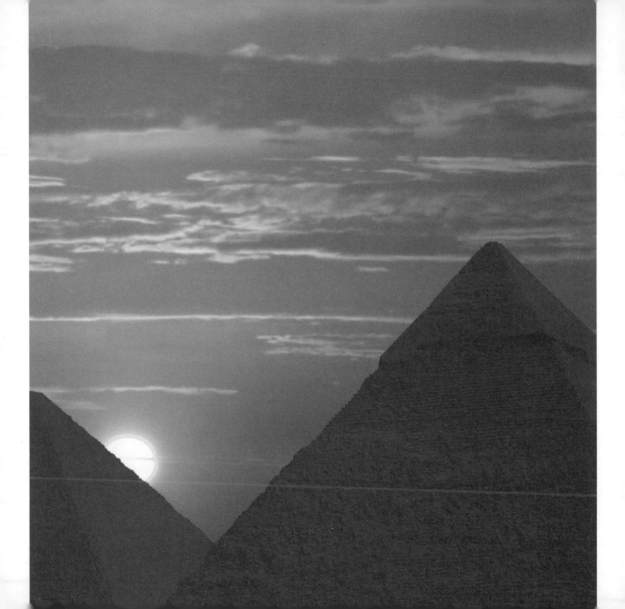

The Egyptians quickly discovered that Natron could also be used as an extremely effective cleaner around the home. Not only that, but blended with olive oil it made soap; in its natural state, it could be used as toothpaste and diluted it made a breath-freshening antiseptic mouthwash.

What was more, they found that Natron burned with a smokeless flame when mixed with castor oil – handy for working in tombs without leaving soot stains. And it was useful in chemical processes such as glass making. All in all a pretty remarkable and versatile substance.

Then Came Pearl Ash and Soda Ash

Over the centuries, the various elements that make up Natron were refined down to more specific substances for individual uses. Late in the eighteenth century, European pharmacies discovered that another form of sodium, pearl ash, was particularly useful in dramatically speeding up the baking process. However, the production of pearl ash involved the burning of huge amounts of wood to produce ash, and pretty soon wood for pearl ash was in short supply.

In 1791, French pharmacist Nicolas LeBlanc produced a process for turning common salt (sodium chloride) into soda ash (sodium carbonate), a substance with the same characteristics as pearl ash but without the need to burn vast tracts of woodland.

And Finally There Was Baking Soda

American bakers loved soda ash and America was soon producing its own. However, American soda ash could not match the quality of the European product, so American bakers were forced to import large quantities of European soda ash.

All that changed in the 1830s when an American, Austin Church, began experimenting with new ways of producing high-quality sodium bicarbonate. Church, a doctor, developed a process that converted purified sodium carbonate into food-grade sodium bicarbonate.

Giving up his medical practice, Church joined forces with his brother-in-law, John Dwight, moved to New York, and founded John Dwight & Co. Dwight called his sodium bicarbonate 'saleratus' (aerated salt) and was soon selling it to bakers and housewives across the States.

Thirty years later, Austin Church retired from the business a rich man, but he was not finished with sodium bicarbonate.

With his two sons, he set up Arm & Hammer to produce baking soda products, and if you go into any pharmacy or supermarket, you can still find Arm & Hammer toothpaste on the shelves.

You Can Call It:

- baking soda
- bread soda
- bicarbonate of soda (more commonly used in the United Kingdom)
- bicarb (again, more commonly used in the United Kingdom)
- sodium bicarbonate
- saleratus
- or even, sodium hydrogen carbonate

But Do Not Confuse It With:

- caustic soda (sodium hydroxide)
- baking powder (although it does contain baking soda)
- sodium chloride (common salt)
- sodium carbonate (also known as washing soda, or soda ash)

Cleaning

Kitchen

If you glance at the ingredients of most of the cleaning products that live under your sink, you will find a scary list of some truly horrendous-sounding chemicals, many refined from gas and most of them highly toxic. It does not have to be like that. Baking soda used in various ways, neat or diluted, can replace many of those cleaners at a fraction of the price and at considerably less risk to your health. Here's how...

Cleaning Dishes

End that Sinking Feeling

For effective, eco-friendly dish washing, simply add 1 tablespoon baking soda to a sinkful of hot water and swish in the juice of half a lemon. If you use commercial dish-washing liquid, add a couple of tablespoons (or more) of baking soda to the water to boost its action. This is really effective when dealing with greasy dishes.

A Handy Stand-by

Keep a little bowl of dry soda close to the sink. If you encounter a stubborn stain, dip your dishcloth, brush or sponge in and scrub – the offending mark will be gone in a jiffy. This not only works on crockery and pans but is also great for glass and plastic cookware.

 CAUTION: Do not use on nonstick finishes.

And Here's Another One

Pop some baking soda into a flour or sugar shaker and keep it by the sink. Use it to sprinkle on stains, then scrub and rinse. Or recycle a plastic scouring powder or talcum powder container and use to hold dry baking soda. Whatever sort of container you use, be sure to label it carefully so it does not get mistaken for food.

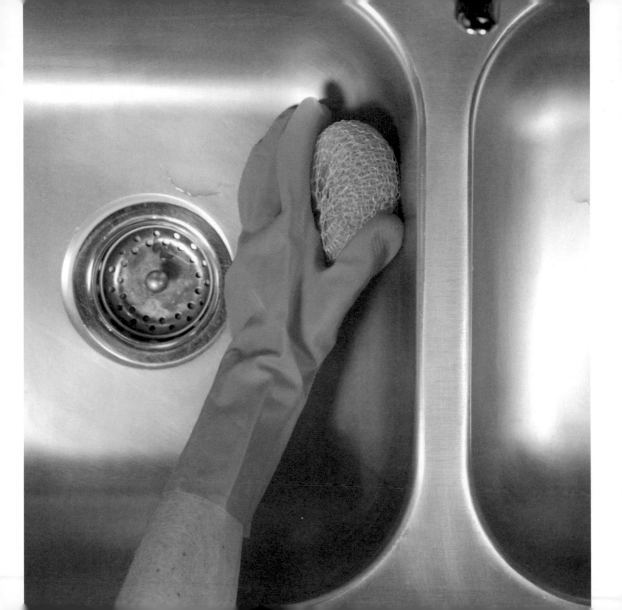

Banish Dirty Dishcloths and Washed-up Sponges

Rinse dishcloths and sponges after use in a solution of hot water and baking soda to keep them smelling like roses. Occasionally soak overnight for an extra powerful freshen-up. Always dry thoroughly before putting away to keep them hygienic and to avoid the build-up of smells.

Up to Your Elbows in Hot Water?

Keep those rubber gloves smelling like daisies by sprinkling a little baking soda into your rubber gloves each time you take them off. Not only will it absorb any dampness and keep them fresh for next time, they will also glide on and off like a dream.

In the Dishwasher

Why spend money on multicolored tablets with a ball stuck in the middle for no apparent reason? Make up your own dishwasher powder by putting 2 tablespoons baking soda and 2 tablespoons borax into the powder compartment for a full load.

To freshen up a whiffy dishwasher and give it a thorough clean, sprinkle about 150 g/5 oz/¾ cup baking soda into the bottom of the machine and run it empty through a complete hot cycle. Whiffiness over. Reduce odor build-up between cycles by sprinkling about a handful of soda over the dirty dishes and on to the bottom of your dishwasher.

For stubborn stains in your dishwasher, use dry soda on a damp cloth or sponge, or mix up a paste with soda and a little water and use like cream cleaner. This is particularly effective for getting rid of those nasty bits that build up around the hinges, rubber door gaskets and in other hard-to-reach areas of dishwashers. Rinse well to remove any residue.

Welcome Home

No one wants to return to a smelly dishwasher after they've been on vacation, so sprinkle a little baking soda into the empty machine and leave the door slightly open. It will be a delight to come back to.

Give Cutting Board Smells the Chop

Cutting boards can acquire a less-than-pleasant smell over time, so give yours a regular spring clean by shaking over about three tablespoons of baking soda and sprinkling with just enough water to moisten. Leave for about 15 minutes to absorb those onion and garlic odors, then rub well with a wet sponge. Rinse in clean water and allow to dry.

Pots and Pans

For those boring things that will not go in the dishwasher, mix together equal quantities of baking soda, borax and salt, and use as a scouring powder that will cut through the heaviest grease and grime on pans, grills and baking trays.

Remember to rinse well afterwards, and do not use on nonstick surfaces, such as Teflon, as it will damage them. Soda will also tend to make aluminium pans go darker.

Don't Want to Wash Them Right Now?

Alternatively, soak dirty pots and pans in a basin of hot water with 2 or 3 tablespoons baking soda for about an hour, then scrub them clean with an abrasive scrubber. Again, not for nonstick under any circumstances.

Left a Pan on the Heat and Forgotten About It?

To remove seriously burned-on food, soak the pan in baking soda and water for 10 minutes before washing, or scrub the pot with dry soda and a moist scouring pad. Do not use abrasive cleaners on nonstick housewares.

For a really scorched pan with burned-on food in the bottom, scrape off as much of the debris as you can, then pour a thick layer of baking soda directly into the pan. Moisten the baking soda with a little water, then leave to work overnight. This should loosen the burnt food and you'll just need to scrub clean and rinse. If this still does not work, boil a strong solution of soda in the pan for about 10 minutes. This should soften up the burnt food sufficiently for you to scrub it away with some dry soda on a damp scourer.

What About Nonstick?

For burnt pans that you don't want to scrub, such as nonstick, bring a mixture of water and 250 ml /8 fl oz/1 cup vinegar to the boil in the pan. Remove from the heat and add a couple of tablespoons of soda. Leave to soak overnight then wipe clean and rinse well.

Mugs and Cups

Use a paste of baking soda and water to remove tea and coffee stains from ceramic and melamine cups. Leave the solution in the cup for a while, then rub and rinse. So much more ecological than bleach, and it does not leave an aftertaste.

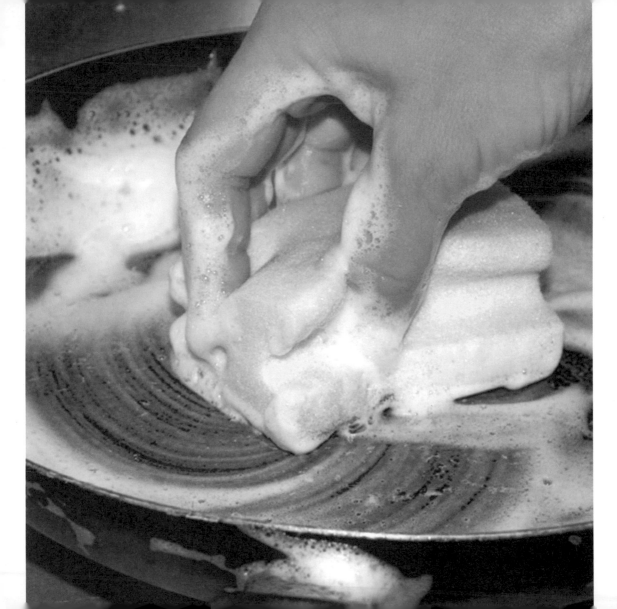

Surfaces

Work on those Worktops

Wipe your kitchen worktops over with a little dry baking soda sprinkled on to a damp cloth or sponge. Rinse with clean water and wipe dry. It is a safe and natural way to keep surfaces clean and leaves them free of taint.

Alternatively, mix up a solution of baking soda and hot water and use this to wash down your worktops, leaving them sparkling and fresh. Rinse and dry as above. Rinse your cleaning cloths or sponges in the same solution and dry thoroughly before putting away.

Freshen up Formica

To erase stains on laminate worktops such as Formica, use a thick paste of baking soda and rub gently until the offending mark disappears. Rinse well. If that does not fix it, squeeze some lemon juice on to the stain, leave for around half an hour, then add a little dry soda to the lemon. Rub with a sponge, rinse clean and dry.

Shining Sinks

Sinks come up sparkling and bright when you clean them with baking soda. Use dry on a damp cloth, or make up a paste with soda and water, and use like cream cleaner.

Degrease Lightning

Prevent the build-up of grease in your kitchen sink drain by regularly putting a large handful of dry baking soda down. Do this about once a month for best results, and make sure you do it just before you set off on vacation so there are no nasty drain smells on your return.

Alternatively ...

Keep your sink drain fresh by regularly putting a handful of baking soda down the plug with the same amount of salt, and follow it down with a cupful of boiling water. Leave for about half an hour, then pour down a whole kettleful of boiling water.

Back to White

If your porcelain or white enamel sink has taken on an unpleasant yellowish tinge, get it looking like new by mixing 1 litre warm water with 50 g/2 oz/¼ cup soda and 120 ml/4 fl oz/ ½ cup chlorine bleach. Pour into the sink and leave to soak for quarter of an hour.

 CAUTION: Keep children and pets away while you are doing this. Rinse well until the bleachy smell goes completely.

Dispense with Dirty Waste Disposals

Keep waste disposal units clean by switching the unit on and running hot water through it. While it is still running, add a handful of soda, then keep the faucet running until all traces of powder have disappeared.

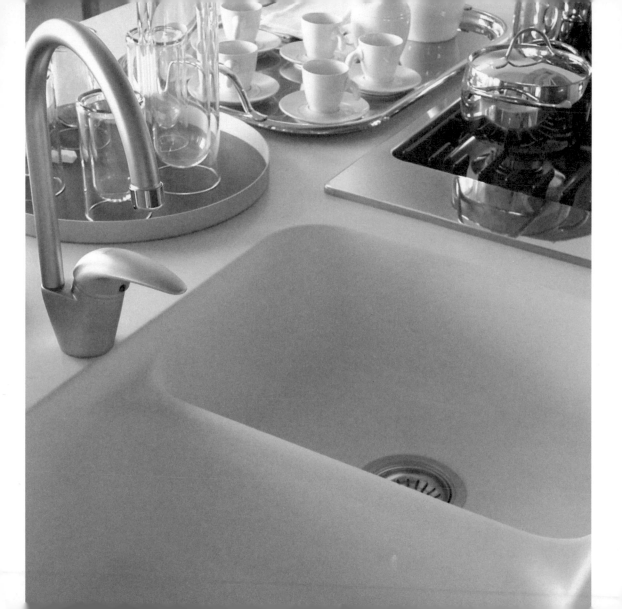

Appliances

Top Cook-top Tip

Make a paste of soda and water and use like all-purpose cleaner on a sponge or cloth. Wipe over well to remove all streaks and rinse with clean water. Alternatively, dampen the stove top and sprinkle with soda. Leave for half an hour to absorb any grease, then rub clean and rinse well. Wipe over glass burners with a solution of hot water and baking soda on a sponge or cloth. Tackle any stubborn marks or burned-on food with dry baking soda on a wet cloth.

Detox Your Oven Cleaner and Your Oven

Proprietary oven cleaners can be highly toxic, and often contain caustic chemicals that give off dangerous fumes. Not nice. However dirty your oven is inside, baking soda can beat the burned-on grime. Scrape off as much gunge as you can, then mix plenty of baking soda with a little water to make a thick paste. Spread this over the sides and bottom of the cold oven and leave overnight. Wipe down the next day with hot water and repeat if necessary. Use dry baking soda on a scourer or sponge to deal with really stubborn areas, rinsing well afterwards.

Oven Spritzer

Another way to keep ovens fresh and clean is to spray the interior of the oven with water (a plant or laundry sprayer works well for this), then sprinkle with dry baking soda. Spray again to dampen the powder. Give further spritzes with water every hour or so, leave the mixture overnight and then remove with a cloth. Rinse with hot water.

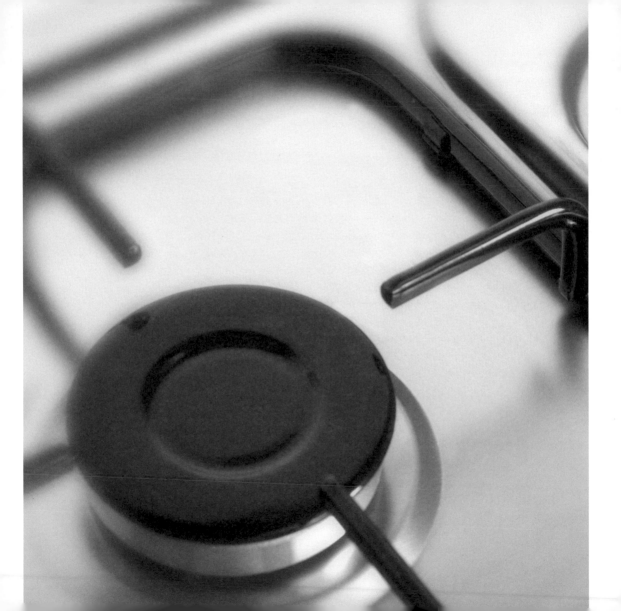

Can't See through that See-through Door?

Glass oven doors can get so splattered with grease and grime that you cannot see through them any more. Get them crystal clear again by scrubbing with baking soda on a damp cloth or sponge. Rinse well and dry.

Microwave Maxi Cleaning

Insides of microwaves can get sprayed with over enthusiastically heated food, leaving them smelling musty, especially when the door is kept closed. To refresh your microwave without leaving any taint or chemical smells, remove the turntable plate if there is one, and wash this in the sink in a solution of hot water and baking soda, then dry. Wipe over the inside of the microwave with a solution of 1 1/2 pts/1 qt hot water and 4 tablespoons baking soda. Be sure to wring your cloth or sponge out well before wiping, as you don't want water to get into the workings through any little perforations in the inside of the oven.

Tackle stubborn splashes with dry baking soda on a damp cloth or sponge and rinse clean. Dry the inside of the microwave and replace the turntable. You can wipe down the outside using the same solution.

More Microwave Magic

Another way to freshen your microwave is to add a couple of tablespoons of baking soda to a half-full cup or mug of hot water (make sure the cup or mug is microwave-safe). Put in the oven on full power and boil for around five minutes. The steam will condense on the inside of the warm oven, loosening splatters of food and leaving it damp. All you need to do is wipe over with kitchen paper, a cloth or sponge, and then dry.

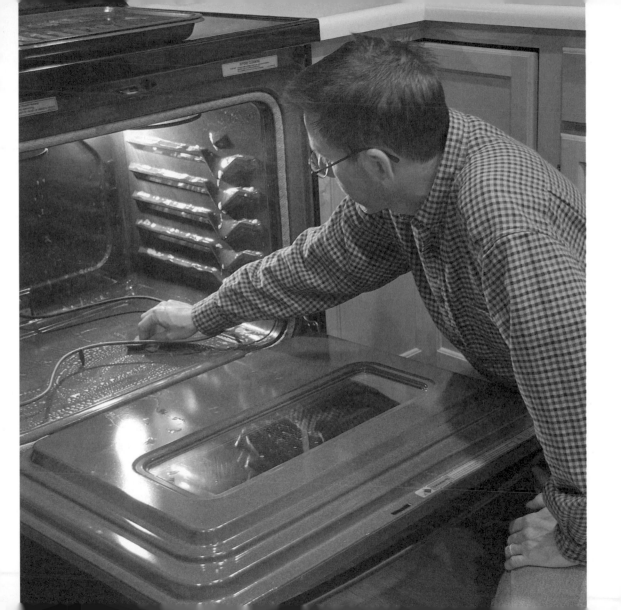

Freshen up Your Fridge

Fridges need a complete spring clean every now and again, especially if something has gone off in there and the smell just will not go away. Remove all the food, shelves, drawers and containers, and wipe them over, along with all surfaces and nooks, with a solution of hot water and baking soda on a clean cloth or sponge (an old toothbrush is useful for difficult crannies, and you can use dry powder on the wet brush for stubborn marks). Rinse and dry carefully before switching the appliance back on.

If you need to leave a fridge switched off, leave the door propped open and pop an open container of baking soda inside.

And Don't Forget the Freezer

If you have to defrost your freezer, wipe it over inside with a solution of 4 tablespoons baking soda to 1 1/2 pts/1 qt warm water. Wipe over all surfaces and dry before turning the freezer back on.

If your freezer is frost-free, it can be tempting to leave it for eons without cleaning it. But even frost-free freezers appreciate a wipe down inside from time to time. Use the same solution as above.

Clean on the Inside, Clean on the Outside

Kitchen appliances, cookers, fridges, burners and so on can get amazingly grimy when you're not looking. Wipe the whole lot over regularly using a solution of baking soda and warm water. Use a cloth or sponge and wring out to avoid drips.

Odor Removal

Fridge (Odor) Magnet

Strong cheese is great, but things like that can leave a not-so-great smell in the fridge. Fight back by leaving an open container of baking soda in there to absorb strong smells and eliminate stale odors. Stir the contents regularly and replace every two or three months or you will find the baking soda itself is starting to pong!

A Fresher Salad Crisper

While you're dealing with the fridge, sprinkle the bottom of the salad drawer with a little dry baking soda, then cover with a layer of kitchen towel. Wipe out and change every three months.

'Vacuum' Your Flask

Get rid of musty or unappetizing smells in a vacuum flask simply by adding a teaspoonful of baking soda, filling it with hot water, then leaving it to soak for at least 30 minutes. Empty and rinse well with cold water. Leave the top off if you're not going to use it for a while.

And a Fresher Air Freshener

Fill a small bowl almost to the top (choose a pretty one for added effect) with baking soda and add a few drops of your favorite essential oil. Place anywhere in the house that you need

to keep things smelling sweet. Add more oil when the effect starts to wane and replace the whole lot about every three months.

When it is not convenient to have an open bowl around (such as under a sink), cut the feet off a clean old pair of tights and fill the foot with soda. Knot the leg and place this inside the other cut-off foot. Knot this again and put it anywhere you need to eliminate stale smells.

Smelly Hands?

If you have just been chopping onions or garlic, peeling potatoes or handling fish, it can be difficult to erase the smell, even with soap. Baking soda will get rid of the whiff – sprinkle some on to wet hands, rub together well and rinse off.

Onion Odor Eaters

Remove the odor of onion and garlic from wooden or other porous surfaces by sprinkling some baking soda on to a damp cloth and rubbing it into the surface. Rinse with water, or leave for about half an hour to work for stronger smells.

Plastic Food Boxes

Plastic can absorb strong smells and less-than-appetizing odors can build up in plastic food boxes, especially if they are left closed or were not scrupulously clean when put away. Banish those musty odors by washing the container in a hot water and baking soda solution, then sprinkle about 3 tablespoons of soda into the base of the container and top up with hot water. Put the lid on and shake gently over the sink, then leave for at least a couple of hours to work. Rinse out and wash again as usual.

Seasonal Smells

Musty smells can build up in food containers that are only used during certain times of the year. To prevent this, sprinkle the insides of picnic hampers and cool boxes with a little baking soda before putting away. Wipe out with a damp cloth before using.

Ban Smelly Trash Cans

If your kitchen trash can has a permanent pong, make a solution of 200 g/7 oz/1 cup baking soda in warm water. Pour it in and top up with more warm water. Leave it to soak for an hour or two, then empty down a drain or the toilet. Make sure you rinse and dry carefully, as bacteria and mould (the cause of bad smells) multiply much faster in warm, steamy conditions.

To prevent smells building up in the first place, sprinkle a little baking soda in the bottom of the can, then line the base with a couple of sheets of newspaper, before inserting a (biodegradable) trash can liner.

If a liner leaks, do not ignore it. Deal with it right away by wiping out the can with a baking soda solution and rinsing with clean water. Change the newspaper and baking soda regularly, every month or so, to keep things really fresh.

And Bread Box Mould

Accumulated crumbs in the bottom of a bread box can easily turn mouldy (ugh). Make sure you tip them out regularly and wipe over the inside of the box with a solution of baking soda and warm water. Remember to dry the box out thoroughly and allow it to cool before you place fresh bread in it, or the mould will return.

Bathroom

The bathroom is a place to pamper yourself as well as keep clean, so it is really important that you keep it spotless and germ-free. And because they are often damp and steamy, bathrooms easily attract mildew and mould, and no one wants to stare at those when they're soaking in the tub. As your skin comes into contact with the surfaces, the bathroom is the last place you want to use toxic chemicals for cleaning, so it's time to reach for that tub of baking soda again.

General

All-over Clean

For general bathroom cleaning, including the bath, basin, shower tray and wall tiles, mix a paste of baking soda and water and use it like cream cleaner on a damp cloth or sponge.

Get rid of more stubborn stains with dry baking soda on a damp cloth or sponge. Rinse well to remove any streaks and wipe dry.

Sweet Smells

Baking soda is perfectly safe for all surfaces, and a couple of drops of essential oil added to the cleaning mix will add extra freshness, so no need for harmful air sprays. Give lemon, pine, tea tree or ylang ylang a try.

Grimy Nonslip Strips?

Nonslip strips are a useful safety measure but difficult to keep looking spotless. You will find they get dingy after a while, which may also make them less effective. The answer? Wet the strips and sprinkle with baking soda. Leave to work for about half an hour, then rub clean with a sponge or cloth and rinse well. Job done.

Say Goodbye to Bathroom Odors

Musty smells can lurk in bathroom cabinets and cupboards, particularly under basins where there might be slight leakage from pipes and faucets. Keep your bathroom storage areas smelling fresh by putting a small open container of baking soda in each one; this will also help absorb damp.

If you use baking soda as an air freshener in your bathroom, remember to replace it about every three months, but don't throw it in the trash – tip it down the toilet, leave for a while, then flush, and you'll get extra value from it.

Leaving an open bowl of baking soda outside the bathroom or by the toilet will help to absorb any nasty niffs. Choose a pretty container that goes with the room scheme and, again, replace the contents about every three months. Add a few drops of essential oil for a luxurious touch.

Banish Musty Bathroom Trash Cans

Bathroom trash cans can quickly get a bit musty, which is both unhygienic and unpleasant. If yours is washable, rinse it clean with a solution of baking soda and dry carefully. Whether washable or not, all will benefit from a sprinkle of soda in the bottom, covered with a square of kitchen towel. Tip or wipe out the powder about every three months and replace the paper as necessary.

Bathroom Hardware

Tap Dancing

If you live in a hard-water area, there's a good chance that there is a limescale deposit around the taps on the faucet – annoying and hard to shift. Not any more – mix some baking soda with a little vinegar and brush the fizzy paste on the offending areas. Leave for about half an hour, then rub gently and rinse clean. This works equally well for all hard-water marks in the bathroom, including on glass shower screens.

Keep Your Drains Running Clear

Regular drain cleaning helps minimize unpleasant smells and guards against blockages. Keep your drains clear by mixing two parts baking soda, two parts salt and one part white vinegar and pouring the solution down the plugholes in your bath, basin and shower. Put in the plugs and leave the mixture to froth away merrily for about half an hour, then run the hot faucet to rinse. Easy.

Bath Time

Baking soda is safe for cleaning all types of baths, but you probably don't always want the bother of cleaning it straight after you've had a soak. No problem: just sprinkle a couple of tablespoons of baking soda into the bathwater before you pull out the plug and your bath will be as clean as you are.

Shower Power

Any type of shower cubicle can be cleaned quickly and effectively with baking soda-and-water paste. If you're feeling lavish, add a little shampoo or shower gel to the mix for a nice smell.

If you live in a hard-water area, you will know that glass shower doors soon get covered in annoying water marks. Don't worry: just wipe the glass over with a little white vinegar on a cloth or sponge and then rub over with a sprinkle of baking soda. Rinse well and then squeegee the glass for streak-free spotlessness you can be proud of. Keep a squeegee in the shower and get all the family to have a quick run over the surfaces with it after each shower. It will cut down on cleaning enormously.

Clear Your Head

Another common problem in hard-water areas is blocked showerheads – not what you need first thing in the morning. If you are able to remove the head, soak it in a mixture made up of 250 ml/8 fl oz/1 cup vinegar with 3 tablespoons baking soda in a suitable container slightly bigger than the head, until the limescale has completely dissolved.

If for any reason you cannot remove the head to clean it, tip the baking soda-and-vinegar mixture into a strong plastic bag, a little bigger than the showerhead, and tie or tape it in place over the head so it is in close contact with the frothy solution. Leave in place for the mixture to work its magic for about half an hour, then remove the bag and rinse the head with clean warm water. Run water through the head to clear any residue and you will soon be singing in the shower again.

Curtains for Mouldy Shower Curtains

A mouldy shower curtain is the last thing you want flapping around when you're trying to get clean. Soak yours regularly in warm water with about 5 tablespoons baking soda (the bath is a good place for this). Give it a slosh around a few times, then squeeze out and hang to drip dry. Always let shower curtains dry flat after washing, otherwise you will find the mould will be back again. Not nice.

For mouldy patches or stubborn stains, make up a thick paste of baking soda and rub clean using a sponge, cloth, old nailbrush or toothbrush.

Machine-washable shower curtains can be laundered on the gentle setting with about 100 g/3½ oz/½ cup baking soda or half that amount of mild washing powder and the same of baking soda. Throw in a couple of towels to absorb suds and water, and help wash the curtain (which is probably waterproof!) more effectively. Adding 250 ml/8 fl oz/1 cup white vinegar to the rinse cycle will help.

 CAUTION: Do not use the spin cycle or you could end up with a permanently creased curtain (and shower curtains are not usually designed to be ironed). Drip

dry instead in an airy place (outside is ideal) or hang it back up in the shower and leave the window open.

Be Kind to Your Toilet

Proprietary toilet cleaners use harsh, caustic chemicals such as bleach, which can stain your clothes if it splashes, harm your hands and, of course, end up in the water supply. Be gentle with your toilet: instead, sprinkle some baking soda around the bowl, leave for about half an hour and then scrub with a toilet brush and flush.

Remove more stubborn marks by sprinkling the toilet bowl with baking soda and pouring a dash of white wine vinegar on top. Use a toilet brush to scrub the bowl clean with the bubbling froth that results.

Sitting Comfortably?

Any kind of toilet seat will come up like new when wiped over with a mild solution of baking soda. Don't forget to do the underneath of the seat and lid too. When you have finished, tip the rest of the solution down the toilet for a really thorough clean.

Flushed with Success

Every few weeks, sprinkle some baking soda in your cistern. Leave overnight, then flush the next day for a sparkly clean toilet.

Furnishings & Surfaces

Our homes are under constant attack from dust, germs and bugs, let alone pets, children and the occasional party. Sofas, chairs, curtains and cushions all have to put up with a lot of mistreatment, walls are often on the receiving end of grubby hands (tiny or otherwise!), and floors can suffer from spills and simply from people walking around in shoes designed for the pavement or the park, not the parquet. Bring all these surfaces back to life with a few handfuls of baking soda.

Furniture

Back to White

White and light painted furniture can quickly lose its original brightness. Bring it up like new by wiping faded items over with a solution of 2 tablespoons baking soda to 1 1/2 pts/ 1 qt warm water. Scrub black marks off chair legs with a paste of baking soda and water. Rinse and dry.

Ring the Changes

Get rid of cup rings and other heat marks on wooden furniture by gently rubbing with a baking soda-and-water paste. If this doesn't work, add a pea-sized blob of toothpaste for extra abrasion. Make sure you do not get the furniture wet as this may cause further stains. Wipe over, dry carefully and, finally, buff with some furniture polish.

Dry-clean Your Three-piece Suite in Fifteen Minutes

To give any fabric upholstery a quick dry-clean, sprinkle the surfaces generously with baking soda (use a flour shaker or empty talc container). Leave for about 10 or 15 minutes to absorb any stale odors, then vacuum up all the powder.

Degrease

Annoying grease marks on cloth upholstery can be made to vanish by sprinkling with one part baking soda and one part salt. Simply brush the mixture in lightly with an old toothbrush, then leave overnight to absorb the stain. Vacuum up the next day.

Alternatively ...

Make a paste of 1 tablespoon water and 3 tablespoons baking soda and rub into stains on fabric seat covers – an old toothbrush works well. Leave the mixture to dry, then brush carefully with a clean dry brush and vacuum away any residue.

 CAUTION: It is best to test the mixture first on an inconspicuous area to check that the fabric is colorfast and that it will not affect the surface of the fabric or leave water marks.

A Cure for Under-the-weather Leather and Vinyl

Leather and vinyl furniture often has a textured finish that can trap grease and dirt, leading to a generally grimy effect. Revive the finish by mixing 1 tablespoon baking soda with 250 ml/8 fl oz/1 cup warm water and use on a cloth or sponge to wipe down the furniture. Blast more

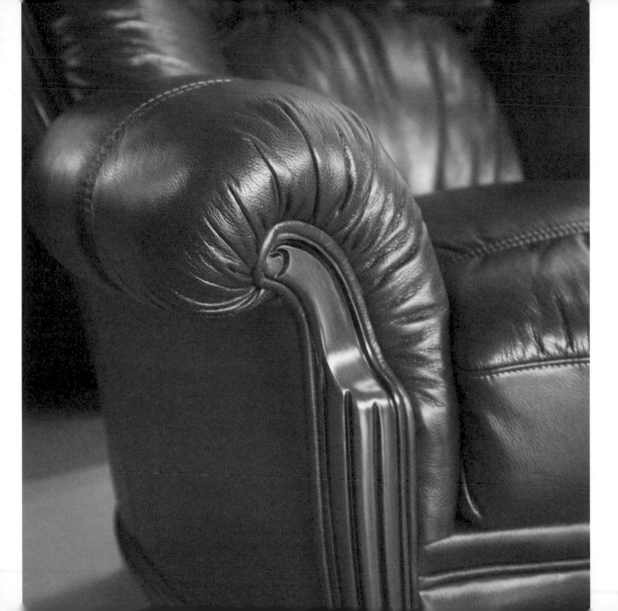

stubborn grime with a paste of baking soda and water. Rubbing this into all the nooks and crannies will leave everything sparkling clean. Wipe over well with clean water on a sponge or cloth and dry.

Metal Furniture

Grimy metal furniture can be brought back to life by cleaning with a paste of baking soda and water on a sponge or cloth. Rinse clean and dry carefully to prevent rust formation.

Rust-buster

If rust does appear on metal furniture, wipe over the affected area with a paste made from 1 tablespoon baking soda and a few drops of water on a damp cloth, then polish with a piece of baking foil and wipe down with a clean damp cloth and dry carefully with kitchen paper.

Lacklustre Laminates?

Any laminate surfaces that are looking a bit off-color will respond well to being spruced up with a damp cloth or sponge sprinkled with baking soda. Rinse and dry.

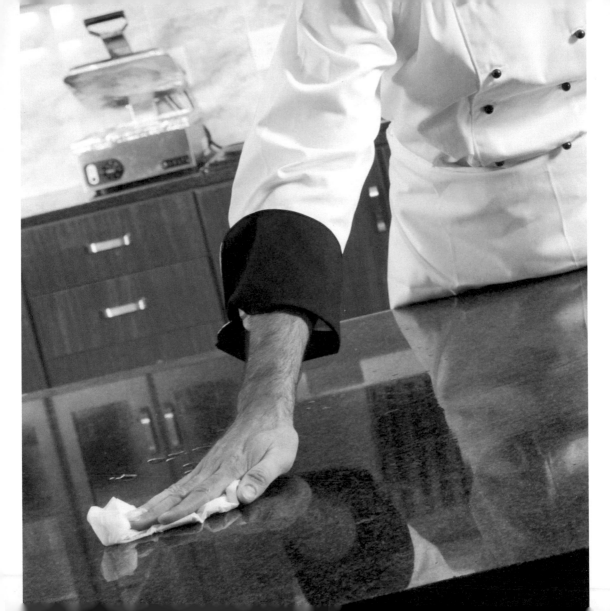

Floors & Walls

All Floors

Looking for an excellent general-purpose hard-floor cleaner that costs pennies? Try dissolving a handful of baking soda in a bucket of warm water and use as normal on a floor mop. Wring out well to avoid saturating the surfaces, then stand back and admire the finish.

Good for Wood

Water can damage parquet and other solid wooden floorings. To remove any offending water marks, take a damp cloth or sponge and sprinkle a little baking soda on to it then rub carefully. Wipe over with a well wrung-out cloth or sponge and dry carefully.

 CAUTION: Do not get the floor wet as this will obviously cause further problems.

Lifeless Linoleum, Vinyl or Cork Floors?

Unsightly scuff marks from dark shoe soles on linolium, vinyl flooring and cork tiles will vanish when rubbed with a paste of baking soda and water.

Crying Over Spilt Ink?

It's no use crying over spilt ink – you just have to do something about it. For spills on hard surfaces, wipe up as much ink as possible, then sprinkle with baking soda. Leave for a few minutes to absorb any residue, then add more powder and rub at the stain with a wet cloth or sponge. For really stubborn stains, moisten the powder with a little vinegar instead of water.

On the Carpet

The sooner you deal with any stain, the better your chance of successfully removing it. This applies just as much to carpets as anything else. If you spill wine or drop grease on your favorite Axminster, sprinkle the area with baking soda (or one part baking soda and one part salt), brush in gently and leave it to absorb the stain for several hours. Sweep up the powder with a clean brush, then dab with a solution of baking soda and warm water. Leave to dry completely, then vacuum the area.

Routine Meaures

If you are going to vacuum the carpet, it will be much fresher afterwards if you sprinkle it with baking soda first. Leave it for about 10–15 minutes, or better still overnight, to work, then vacuum the carpet until all traces of powder have disappeared.

That's Sick

Cleaning up vomit is never a pleasant job, but bring baking soda to the rescue and you can ensure there are no lingering nasty memories. Get your rubber gloves on (sprinkling a little baking soda inside them for freshness and ease of removal) and scrape up as much mess as possible, then cover the area with a layer of baking soda. Leave for a few minutes, then scrub from the edges towards the middle with a sponge or brush moistened repeatedly in clean warm water. Sprinkle the area again with baking soda and leave to dry, then vacuum up the powder. The antibacterial action of baking soda will deal with any residual odors, even on carpet. This process also works well with urine. If you cannot clear up vomit immediately because you're in the middle of an emergency, throw some baking soda over the affected area to curb nasty smells and deal with it as soon as possible.

Removing 'Artwork' from Walls

To clean marks, such as those from crayon, pencil, pens or grease, off washable walls, make a solution of baking soda and warm water and wipe over. If any children's masterpieces or other stains prove hard to shift, sprinkle dry soda on a damp cloth and scour gently.

 CAUTION: It is a good idea to test out on an inconspicuous area of wall first, just in case the finish is not as washable as you thought.

Washable Wallpaper

Rub stains on washable wallpaper with a paste of baking soda mixed with a little water. However, bear in mind there are different kinds of washable, so in case your paper is only 'wipeable' rather than 'scrubbable', always test on a less noticeable part of the wall first.

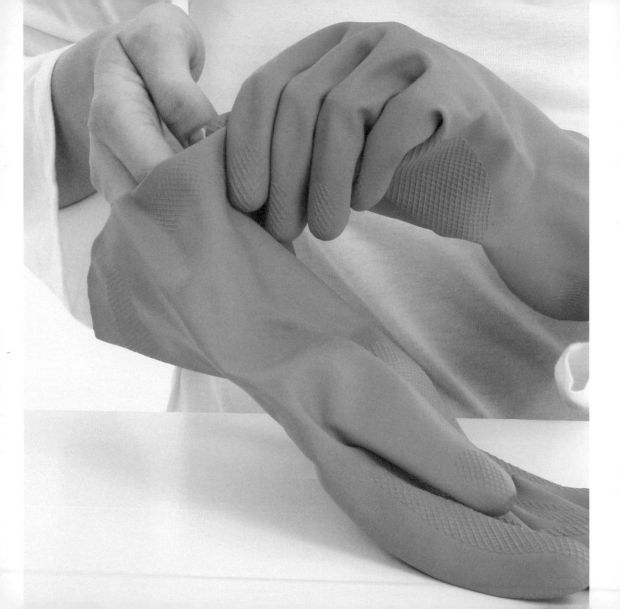

Revive Dull Tiles

Wipe dull, lifeless tiles over with a solution of baking soda, and see them spring back to their old shiny selves. Use the powder dry on a wet cloth or sponge for more stubborn stains and to clear soap residue. When you have finished, rinse with clear water and wipe or squeegee dry.

Defeat Grubby Grouting

Grubby grouting will never show your bathroom in its best light. Revive stained tile grout with a thick paste of baking soda and an old toothbrush. Make sure you rinse the whole area clean when you have finished to remove any white streaks.

Alternatively, for general discoloration on tile grout, make up a fizzy paste using two parts baking soda and one part vinegar or lemon juice. Apply the paste to the grout with an old toothbrush, leave for 10 minutes and then rinse the whole lot off with warm water.

If your grout has really stubborn stains that simply refuse to budge, it's time to use a big gun. Moisten the baking soda with bleach instead of water (but not more than one part bleach to three parts baking soda) and scrub the grout with this, rinsing well afterwards and wiping.

 CAUTION: If you do decide to use the bleach mixture as a last resort, you will need to take a few simple precautions: open the window and wear rubber gloves and old clothes, wash any splashes off your skin immediately, keep the mixture away from children and pets and, of course, make sure you dispose of any leftover mixture safely.

Windows

First Class Glass

It is amazing how dirty windows can get without our noticing. Get in the habit of washing your windows regularly with a wet cloth or sponge sprinkled with a little baking soda. Rinse over with clean water and polish with a crumpled sheet of newspaper until dry, which will help remove any water marks or smears. And don't forget the frames. Wipe them down with a mixture of one part vinegar to two parts baking soda. This is especially effective if condensation has left areas of mildew.

Beautiful Blinds

Washable blinds (do make sure they are washable) will come back to their just-bought glory once you have doused them in a bath of warm water and 250 ml/8 fl oz/1 cup baking soda. Wipe away the dirt with a sponge or dish-washing brush (give the cords a quick scrub too), then rinse down using the shower head or take outside and give a gentle blast with the backyard hose. Hang the blind up to dry.

Mirror, Mirror on the Wall

Like windows, mirrors can quickly lose their lustre. Baking soda is great for bringing up grubby mirrors so they gleam. See yourself in a new light by sprinkling a little baking soda on a damp sponge or cloth and rubbing over the mirror. Wipe over with a clean cloth or sponge and fresh water, then polish with a crumpled newspaper for a sparkling, smear-free finish.

General Household

Wherever the water goes when we empty a sink or bath, or flush the toilet, you can send it swiftly on its way, making sure there are no lingering, unpleasant smells, with a dash of baking soda. Not especially glamorous maybe, but vitally important for our health and wellbeing. And baking soda is great at neutralizing the smell of things around the house, such as shoes, sneakers and pets that are making their presence felt a bit too much.

All-purpose Cleaner

Drain Training

If the water isn't draining away as fast as it normally does, or you suspect you have got a blockage, it's time for action. Pour about 100 g/3½ oz/½ cup baking soda down the sink, swiftly followed by about 120 ml/4 fl oz/½ cup of white vinegar. Put the plug in while the chemicals froth up in a rather satisfying way. Leave bubbling away for a couple of hours, then pour down a kettle of boiling water. Used regularly, this combination will break down the fatty acids that block drains and help to keep them smelling fresh as a daisy.

Going on Vacation?

Don't forget to put a handful of baking soda down all plugholes in the home before you go away for any longer than a couple of days. It will prevent your neighbours suffering any unpleasant bad drain smells while you're gone, especially in hot weather, and it will make your place much nicer for you to come home to.

Sceptical about Septic Tanks?

If you have a septic tank, don't worry. Baking soda is best for keeping it in tiptop shape. In fact, it positively helps the process of breaking down waste by keeping the contents at the correct pH level, which favours the right sort of bacteria. Baking soda helps protect the fabric of the tank from corrosion that can be caused by too-acid an environment. So, if you don't have mains drainage, pop a handful of soda down the toilet each week and give your tank a treat.

Metal Cleaning

Silver Lining

Stop using unpleasant chemicals on your silverware. Instead, banish tarnish by applying a paste of water and baking soda, or dry baking soda on a damp cloth or sponge. Rinse or wipe with clean water and dry.

Adding a tiny squeeze of mild detergent or shampoo to the baking soda paste when you are cleaning the family silver will give you even more cleaning power. Rub, rinse and polish dry.

If you are lucky enough to have some large, flat pieces of silverware, cut a potato in half and dip into a tub of baking soda. Rub over the surface, then polish clean with a soft cloth.

The Family Jewels

You can clean several small items of solid silver jewelry together by placing them in a suitably sized flat glass dish lined with a piece of slightly scrunched-up aluminium foil or baking foil.

Arrange the jewelry on the foil, ensuring each piece is in contact with it. Sprinkle the pieces with baking soda, then boil a kettle of water, let it cool slightly and pour over the items until they are all submerged. Turn the items over gently so all surfaces are in contact with the foil in turn. The tarnish will transfer to the foil. Magic.

Get Stainless Steel and Chrome Really Stainless

Bring any stainless steel and chrome surfaces back to life with a sprinkle of baking soda on a damp cloth or sponge. If you have 'brushed' stainless steel surfaces, these have a grain, so be sure to rub in the right direction. Wipe away any residues with a clean damp cloth and buff up to a good-as-new shine with a dry cloth.

Brassed off with Your Copperware?

Bring copper, brass or bronze up like new by mixing three parts baking soda and one part lemon juice or white vinegar and cleaning with a soft cloth. But remember that if you are polishing brass, you must make sure it is uncoated or it will not work.

Clean copper pans by cutting a plump fresh lemon in half and dipping it in baking soda. Rub the surface of the pan with a circular motion. Wipe clean with fresh water and dry carefully.

The Ring of Confidence

Rings can get clogged up and grimy from daily contact with oily deposits from skin, hand cream, soap or other cosmetics. Bring your precious jewels back to pristine condition by soaking them in a solution made from 1 tablespoon baking soda thoroughly mixed with a cup of tepid water.

 CAUTION: Do not use this method on pearls, or jewelry where the gems may be glued in place rather than set in claws. If in doubt about submerging jewelry, rub gently with a baking soda paste using an old, soft toothbrush. Rinse and dry carefully before putting away.

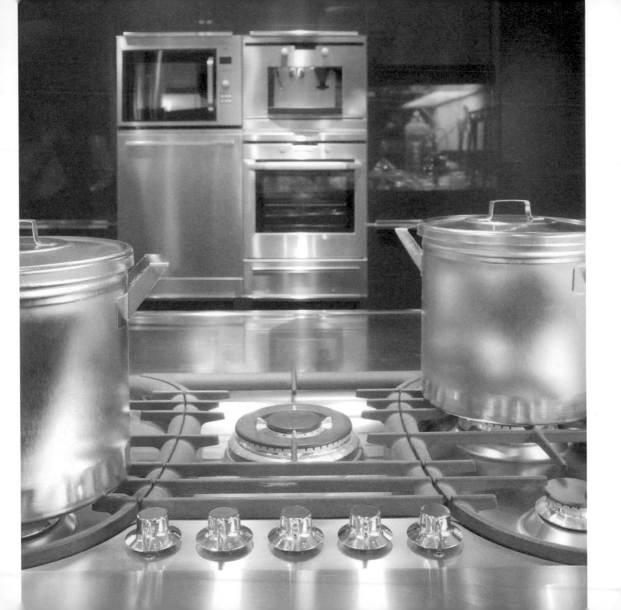

Odor Removal

Whiffy Carpets?

Carpets and rugs can get very musty, especially if you have pets. The solution is to sprinkle with baking soda the night before you vacuum. Sleep sound in the knowledge that the baking soda is hard at work absorbing smells. Vacuum as normal the next day.

Get It off Your Chest

Some people like that evocative *Lion-the-Witch-and-the-Wardrobe* smell that comes from old wooden furniture, but no one likes the way the smell can transfer to clothes, making them feel less than fresh. Banish the smell to Narnia by sprinkling some baking soda in the bottom of the piece of furniture, leave it overnight and vacuum out in the morning, then sprinkle in a bit more and place clean paper over the top.

Banish that dreadful smell of decaying mothballs that hangs about in some ancient furniture by filling a pomander with baking soda, or equal quantities of baking soda and borax, and hanging it up in the wardrobe.

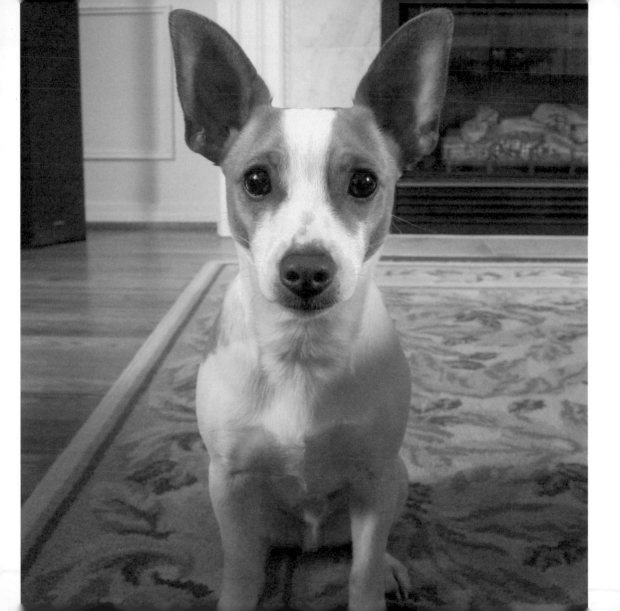

Alternatively ...

If you're feeling creative, or short of cash, make a sachet from old clean tights, or fill a small container and stand it in the corner of the cupboard. Well-washed plastic food containers, or small sturdy cardboard boxes with holes punched in the lid, filled with baking soda, are ideal. Having a lid makes it less likely to get tipped over and spilt.

Blanket Measures

If blankets smell musty when you take them out of storage, sprinkle them with baking soda and fold them up. Leave them overnight, then shake out in the backyard and hang in the sunshine, or give them a 20-minute twirl in the tumble dryer on a low setting.

A Bed of Roses

Mattresses can get fusty, especially if not used for a while – not a pleasant place to lay your head. Get rid of the fug by removing the mattress cover if there is one, dusting the mattress with soda and leaving it overnight before vacuuming it up. Turn the mattress over and repeat the process. Add a further sprinkling of baking soda before you put back the mattress cover (which you've washed!) and make up the bed. Pillows will benefit from the same treatment.

Butt Out

If you're a smoker, sprinkling a layer of dry baking soda in your ashtrays offers a double whammy. Not only does it absorb unpleasant smoky odors, but it also works as a fire-extinguisher, so helps put smouldering butts out. Unfortunately it won't do anything about cleaning up your lungs.

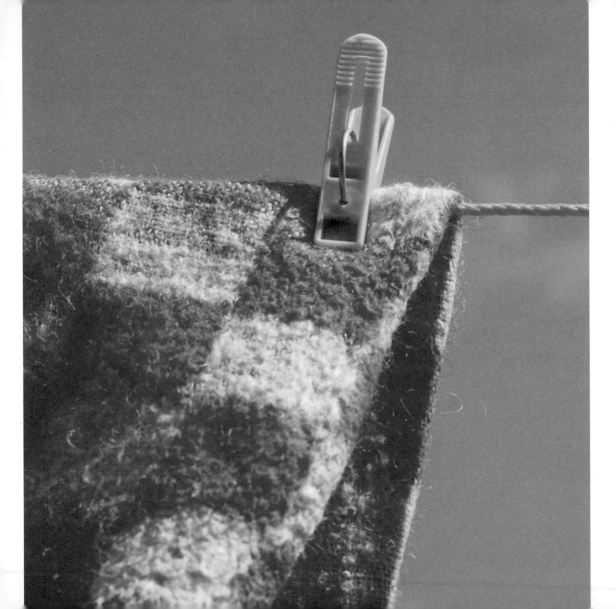

Fusty Footwear

Let's face it, sneakers, shoes, boots and slippers can start to smell horrible if not taken care of properly. Avoid embarrassing stink-foot by sprinkling a couple of tablespoons of baking soda into each shoe and shaking carefully to distribute throughout its whole length. Tip down the toilet before wearing to keep your toilet smelling fresh as well.

For a potentially less messy solution, make sachets to go in your shoes to keep them fresh. The simplest way is to pour some baking soda into the foot section of old tights, knot at the ankle and trim. Pop one in each shoe when you're not wearing them.

Sprinkling a bit of baking soda on your feet (and in your socks) before you put your shoes on will help deal with footwear odor at the source if you are prone to this problem.

Game, Set and ... Smell

Sports and swimming bags can smell truly ghastly if they are not kept aired and free of dirty or wet kit. Avoid the shame of stinky kit-bagitis by sprinkling the inside of the emptied bag with baking soda. Leave it overnight, then vacuum out. Sprinkle a bit more in the bottom and leave it there to absorb moisture and bad odors. If you are a member of a sports club with your own locker, it will stay fresh and much more civilized if you pop a small open container of baking soda in the corner.

Upstairs, Downstairs

Attics, lofts, basements and cellars often have a characteristically damp, fusty smell. Tights to the rescue again: cut the legs off and fill the foot section with baking soda. Add another

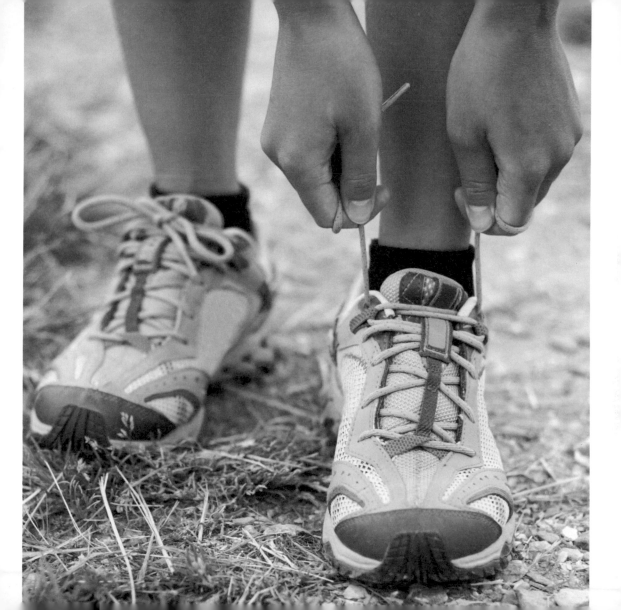

layer of tights to make double thickness and then knot firmly. Use the rest of the leg to make a loop and attach it to a rafter, beam or hook. It might look odd (actually, it does look odd) but it does the trick.

Love Your Luggage

Suitcases, trunks, travel bags and other items of luggage often get stored for months at a time and can get a musty smell, especially when left in the loft or attic. When you get your luggage down for a trip, sprinkle a little baking soda inside the day before you pack, leave overnight and vacuum thoroughly in the morning.

If spots of mildew appear on superior-looking leather luggage that has been left in storage or damp conditions, bring it back to its rightful position in life by gently rubbing the affected areas with a paste of baking soda and water. Dry off with a clean cloth, leave to dry thoroughly, then buff up with a suitable colored polish.

Tame that Tome

Old books can be yet another source of unpleasant musty odors. Use an old librarian's trick once you're sure the book is dry, and sprinkle lightly throughout with baking soda. Leave the book for a few days, then shake out the powder. The result: a book it is a pleasure to get your nose stuck into again.

Accidental water spills can cause the pages of books to buckle and stick together, but don't despair. Dry out wetness (or dampness) on paper by sprinkling the affected pages with baking soda and leave the book to dry in a sunny window or the airing cupboard, turning the pages regularly.

Pets

We all love our pets; that's a given. But sometimes they can smell less than fragrant, and occasionally they disgrace themselves when we're not looking. Wet dogs, cat litter and hamster cages all have their unique aroma and it's not one that adds to the pleasure of relaxing at home. Reach for the baking soda and they will soon be your best friends again.

Bathing & Floors

Washing, Wet or Dry

Give your pooch a quick dry-clean by sprinkling him (or her, of course) with a little baking soda and brushing it through the coat. Probably best done in the backyard, this will absorb grease and remove those doggy smells you do not want to smell.

For a wet wash, add a couple of tablespoons of baking soda to the water when you bathe your dog. This solution can be used by itself, when it will also help heal any skin conditions, or with a dash of shampoo. You will not need to use as much shampoo as usual, as the addition of baking soda makes it work much more effectively. Rinse thoroughly after shampooing.

A Cleaner Vacuum Cleaner

Every time you change the bag in your vacuum cleaner pop in 1 tablespoon soda. And if it's the bagless type just drop the baking soda into the dirt collection chamber. This will quickly curb that less-than-fresh smell that can linger when the cleaner starts to get full, especially if you have a dog in the house.

Whoops

When man's best friend leaves a nasty niff on the carpet, sprinkle on some baking soda. Leave it for half an hour, then vacuum up. The baking soda will also help stop those doggy smells gathering in your vacuum cleaner.

Worse Than Whoops

After a night on the tiles, or swallowing too much fur, your cat can sometimes be sick and will seldom, if ever, use the litter tray. Wherever your cat decides to throw up, a solution of baking soda and water will not only clean up the mess, it should also remove any stains and unpleasant smells.

The Worst

Should one of your pets leave something unspeakable on the carpet, scrape up or dry up as much as you can, then scrub the whole area with a solution of baking soda and warm water. Sprinkle the area liberally with more baking soda and leave overnight, vacuuming up any residue the next day.

Getting rid of that telltale smell quickly will discourage the little darlings from soiling the same spot repeatedly.

Pets' Accessories

Kitty Litter

With the best will in the world, most of us do not manage to clean out litter trays quite as often as we should. Luckily, baking soda will absorb those telltale cat litter odors if you plan ahead. Next time you change your cat's tray, cover the bottom with a layer of baking soda and then sprinkle the cat litter on top. Be generous with the baking soda: the best arrangement is a ratio of around one part baking soda to four parts of litter. Add a little extra soda each time you remove anything between changes.

And So to Bed

Pets' beds and bedding can get dirty and start to smell. Freshen up your pet's sleeping arrangements by sprinkling with soda, leaving for at least 10 minutes, then vacuuming.

Pet blankets can be home to some particularly powerful odors that even a good hot wash won't always shift. Bring your blankets back to smell-free cleanliness by adding 100 g/3½ oz/½ cup baking soda to the detergent, either for machine or hand washing.

White-collar Pets

Dogs' collars and leashes can get grimy and greasy over time, so scrub with a solution of baking soda and warm water. Nylon collars and leashes can be soaked in the solution if you prefer. This also works well on those plastic toys that your pet loves gnawing on.

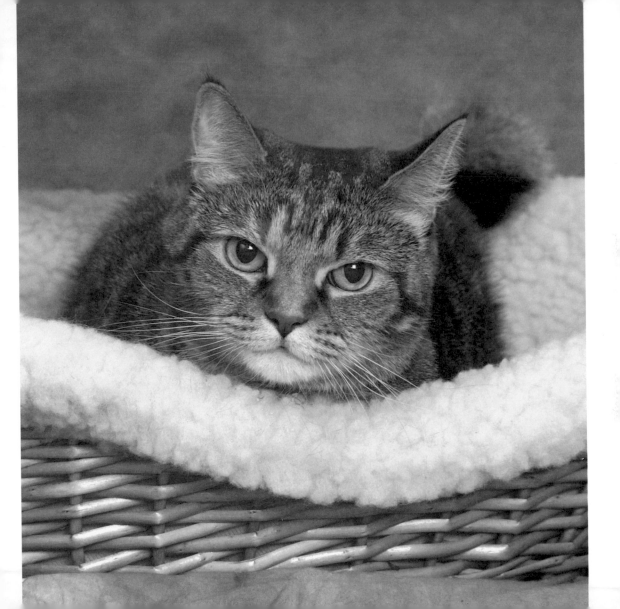

How Clean Is Your Cage?

Next time you clean out a small pet's cage, sprinkle a layer of baking soda on the bottom before covering with a layer of newspaper, then bedding. Tank-style cages can be washed out with a solution of baking soda and warm water and rinsed in the bath or shower.

Feathered Friends

Birds can get salmonella and other similar gastric problems if you do not keep their feed hoppers and drinking containers spotless.

Wash these carefully in a hot water and baking soda solution and rinse and dry carefully before replacing. Use the same solution, rather than strong-smelling detergent, to clean out the cage.

Thanks for All the Fish (Tank)

Fish do not like it if their water becomes too acidic, so test the water with a special kit regularly and add a pinch or so of baking soda to correct the level if necessary. And when you need to clean the tank, baking soda and water in paste form is perfect for scrubbing it out. It is safe and leaves no taint.

 CAUTION: Make sure you rinse the tank out carefully before refilling.

Laundry

Clean & Condition

Sparkling clean, sweet-smelling and soft laundry is one of life's pleasures. But as manufacturers compete to bring us cleaner, brighter, whiter, fresher laundry at lower temperatures, they simply add more and more chemicals to their powders. In the long run, this leads to fabrics not lasting as long and an increasing number of people finding they are allergic to washing powders. Baking soda is a simple, inexpensive solution – its mildly alkaline content means it dissolves dirt and grease, leaving laundry soft and clean.

Cleaning Clothes

Painless Stain Removal

Any type of stain is always best dealt with before it has time to dry because once the mark starts to set it will become much more difficult to remove. Because of its unique formulation, baking soda is great for many types of stain removal as well as for laundry.

 CAUTION: To be on the safe side, always test stain removal techniques on an inconspicuous area of the material first, especially if it is a favorite item of clothing.

Blood Simple

Blood stains are always difficult to remove, as anyone who watches crime TV shows will tell you. Baking soda, however, will normally remove blood from washable clothing.
For small areas of blood, dampen the stain with cold water, but not hot water as this sets blood stains, making them far more difficult to remove. Rub baking soda into the stained area with an old toothbrush or clean nailbrush. Leave the baking soda paste on to soak for a while and repeat the process if necessary. Launder as normal.

Blood Not So Simple

For larger areas of blood, add 200 g/7 oz/1 cup baking soda and 250 ml/8 fl oz/1 cup white vinegar to a bucket of cold water. Swirl the mixture around well and then add the bloodstained clothing. Leave for several hours – overnight is ideal – then launder as usual.

Vomit and Urine

There is no nice way to say this, but vomit and urine are acidic. The first thing to do is thoroughly rinse any stains under a cold faucet as soon as possible after the event to avoid lasting damage to the fabric. Sprinkle the area with baking soda and leave for about half an hour before washing. Baking soda will neutralize the acid and prevent it from permanently damaging clothing.

For larger areas of vomit, scrape off as much as you can, then soak the item or items in a bucket of cool water to which you have added 200 g/7 oz/1 cup baking soda.

Couldn't Face Cleaning It at the Time?

If acidic stains or spills have dried on to clothes, do not soak them in water as the acid will be reactivated and will start to harm the clothes. This explains why clothes that have had acid splashed on them go into the wash intact and come out with holes. Instead, mix some baking soda with a little water and spread on to the stain. This will neutralize the acid before it has time to start eating into the fabric. Leave the baking soda on for an hour or two, then wash as normal. This also works for other acid spills such as lemon, orange and other citrus juices (which, although they are good for you, are acidic), acidic toilet cleaners and battery acid. You can also try this for wine spills and other fruit stains.

No Sweat!

Scrub those unpleasant perspiration stains from washable clothing with a nailbrush and a paste of baking soda and water, leave for at least an hour to work effectively, longer for bad stains, then wash as normal. Not only will this remove the stain, it will get rid of the smell too.

Ease off Grease

Grease stains can be so frustrating. They just seem to come back wash after wash. Don't despair: sprinkle fresh grease splashes with soda and leave for an hour or two to work, then drip a little water on to the powder and scrub gently. Rinse off and wash as normal.

For dry-clean only clothes, just sprinkle the dry powder on as above, leave to work and brush off with a clean soft brush.

Ballpoint Blobs?

Ballpoint pen or other types of ink can be removed from leather clothing, but you need to act fast. Sprinkle a little baking soda on the stain, leave for a couple of hours to absorb the ink, then brush off and buff up the leather.

Grey-collar Worker?

Greasy, discolored collars and cuffs will get short shrift if you scrub them with a paste of soda and water and a nailbrush. Leave to soak for half an hour, then wash as normal.

For severe stains, try drizzling a little white vinegar on to the soaking mixture. The resulting froth will deliver the extra grease-busting power that you need.

Persuade Suede to Come Clean

Suede is all too easy to stain and expensive to dry-clean. Before you head to the cleaners, try gently rubbing dry baking soda into stains on suede, using a soft brush. Leave it to set,

then brush off carefully. It makes sense to try this on an inconspicuous part of the garment before you proceed to ensure it does not have any adverse effects.

New Baby, New Clothes

New baby clothes often contain a dressing that stiffens the fabric so it looks good in the shop. Perversely, this can cause soreness and rashes on delicate baby skin. Rinse this unnecessary chemical concoction out of the clothing before the bambino wears it by washing the offending garment in warm water and a little mild detergent to which you have added 100 g/3½ oz/½ cup baking soda.

Some adults also find their skin is irritated by these fabric dressings, so just follow the same instructions.

Happy Diapers

Disposable diapers can leave a dubious ecological legacy. If you are using the traditional towelling alternative, soak the dirty diapers in baking soda and water overnight. This not only curbs unpleasant smells, but means that you can use less detergent in the machine when it comes to washing them.

In the Swim

Remove damaging chlorine or salt from your bathing costume after a trip to the pool or swimming in the sea by soaking the garment for an hour or two in warm water to which you have added a handful of baking soda. Wash as usual and your swimwear will keep looking good for much longer, and it will not have that worryingly bleachy smell when you next put it on.

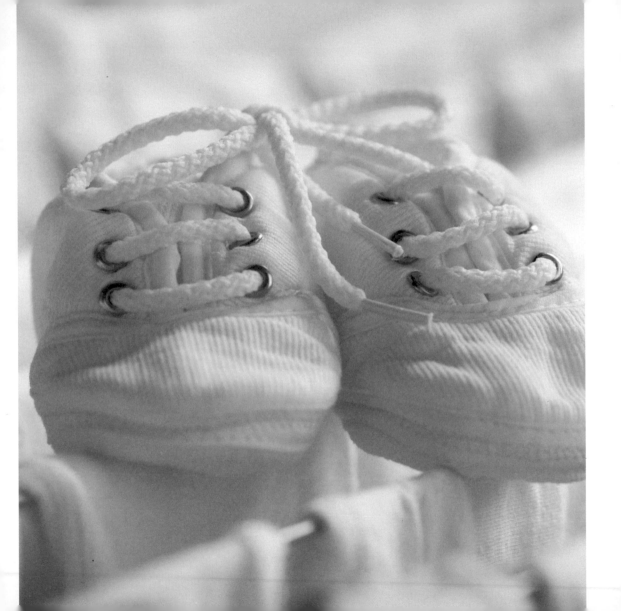

Tune up Your Washing Machine

Adding half a cup of baking soda to a load of washing will improve the performance of your usual liquid detergent. And, as it acts as a very effective water softener, you will find you get the same results with considerably less detergent than usual. What's more, your white clothes will come out looking whiter, and brightly coloured clothes will keep their colour longer.

Reduce Rashes

If, in common with many people, you are allergic to commercial washing powders and find they irritate your skin, try using 200 g/7 oz/1 cup baking soda in your wash instead. This is also ideal for getting baby clothes lovely and soft.

A Handy Hand-washing Tip

You can hand wash delicate articles in warm water with 50 g/2 oz/¼ cup baking soda and about a tablespoon of hand-washing laundry liquid. Wash and rinse as usual, adding a tablespoon of baking soda to the final rinse as a softener.

 CAUTION: Before you wash anything delicate, you should pay particular attention to the washing instructions that came with the garment.

A Soul Mate for Your Sole-plate

The sole-plate of your iron can easily get marked and hard water will soon block up the steam holes. Remedy this by rubbing over the plate of an unplugged and cool iron with baking soda-and-water paste on a sponge or cloth. Wipe over with a clean damp cloth and buff dry.

Odor Removal

Smoke Gets in Your Clothes

To remove smoke smells from clothes, whether from cigarettes or bonfires, add half a cup of baking soda at the rinse cycle. This will also get rid of the smell of mothballs or musty cupboards that might be lingering on your clothes.

Alternatively, soak smoky clothes in a solution of baking soda before you put them in the washing machine. This works well for clothes tainted with smoke, or clothes that have not been dried properly and have developed that horribly rancid 'old dishcloth' smell.

Perspiration Inspiration

Baking soda not only deals with sweat stains but banishes the smell too. This can be a real boon as work clothes and sports garb can still retain that acrid smell (sorry, there's no nicer way to describe it) even after normal laundering. Soak offending items overnight in a solution of 100 g/3½ oz/½ cup baking soda and 4 l/7 pts/4 qts warm water before laundering as usual.

Pampered Hamper

Banish the whiff of fusty laundry hampers by sprinkling baking soda over the dirty washing. This also prevents the hamper itself from becoming smelly. Add a further handful of baking soda each time you put another load of grubby clothing in.

Popping a home-made sachet into your laundry hamper will absorb unpleasant smells for months. Simply cut out a circle of lightweight fabric, about the size of a dinner plate, and place a large handful of baking soda in the centre. Add some lavender or a few drops of your favorite essential oil. Gather the fabric up around the powder and secure with an elastic band. Tie a ribbon around the band to hang against the side of the hamper or drop it into the bottom. Nice.

Sick Note

Sorry to mention it again, but the smell of sick has a nasty habit of lingering on clothing, even after laundering, so scrape off as much as possible, run the affected area of the garment under the faucet, then sprinkle the area liberally with baking soda and leave to act for about an hour. Scrub and rinse, then launder as normal.

Dunk the Skunk

OK, it's not likely to happen, but if you ever get squirted by a skunk, you will be tempted to put all your clothes in the trash. Stop: you may be able to rescue them if you act quickly. Try soaking the stinky clothes overnight in a solution of 100 g/3½ oz/½ cup baking soda to 4 ½ pts/4 qts water, repeat if necessary, then wash as normal.

Give Your Washing Machine a Break

If you find your washing machine smells less than fresh when you get back from your vacation, sprinkle a little baking soda and leave the door open overnight. Next morning, clean the inside and outside of your washing machine and tumble drier with baking soda sprinkled on a damp cloth or sponge. Next time you go away, sprinkle in the baking soda before you go. No need to rinse out, just leave it in there for the next wash.

Soft & Bright

Soften It Up

Baking soda not only washes clothes, it also works well as a fabric softener. Its gentle action is ideal if you find commercial fabric conditioners irritate your skin, or you want to avoid all that plastic packaging. Try adding 100 g/3½ oz/½ cup soda at the rinse stage or mix with a little warm water and pour into the conditioner drawer. It leaves clothes smelling fresh, but without the artificial perfumed smell of shop-bought softeners. Baking soda as a softener is particularly good for keeping towels fluffy and soft.

Alternatively, mix two parts water, one part baking soda and one part white vinegar. It will fizz up like mad, but once it has calmed down completely you can pour it into a plastic bottle for storage. Be sure to label it clearly and keep it out of the reach of children. Add about 50 ml/2 fl oz/¼ cup of the mixture to the fabric softener drawer in your machine per wash.

Whiter Than White

If you habitually add bleach to the detergent in your washing machine, also add 50 g/2 oz/¼ cup soda if you are using a front-loading machine, or twice as much for top-loaders. Your usual bleach will not only work harder but you will only need to use half the quantity that you usually do. Your white wash will come up brighter, and baking soda is much kinder to your clothes. It is gentle on colored items too. Alternatively, add one part baking soda and one part freshly squeezed lemon juice to your whites wash to get clothes really clean.

Appearance

It is amazing that something as inexpensive as baking soda
can be a boon to everyone who cares about appearance, without having
to pay a fortune. Baking soda can be used in so many different ways
to improve appearance, from alleviating irritating little rashes to making
your skin so healthy-looking that people will believe you have
used one of the luxury brands. Baking soda is so versatile
that you can use it on most parts of your body.

Skin

Soothe Allergic Skin

If you are allergic to anything at all, from food to medication, more often than not the symptoms will show up on the skin in the form of a rash. These skin allergies can often take the shape of unsightly hives, which are very itchy and take ages to disappear.

Although baking soda cannot help with curing the allergy, using it in your bath water can bring enormous relief from the itching. Using 400 g/14 oz/2 cups in a cool bath should be enough to relieve the symptoms, but if you find that particular areas of the body are causing you more intense discomfort, then neat baking soda can be rubbed into these areas for even more relief.

Ease Sunburn and Windburn

In much the same way as baking soda brings relief from allergic skin reactions, 400 g/14 oz/2 cups of

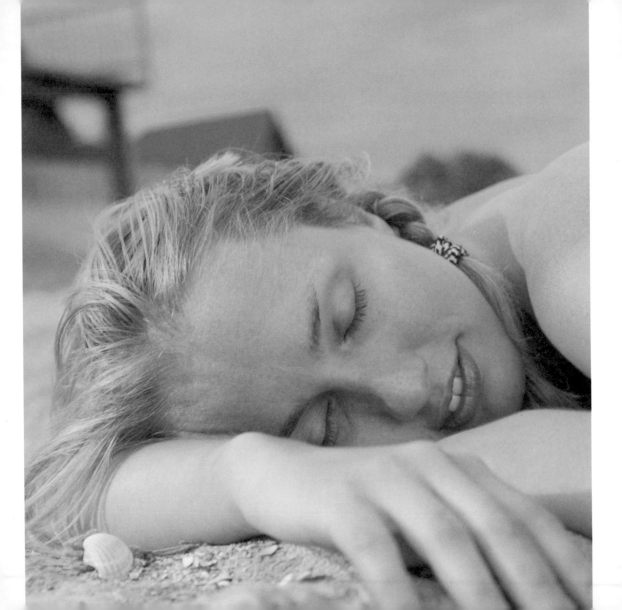

baking soda can also be added to a cool bath if you are suffering from sunburn or have been out in a strong wind for too long. It will help take the burn out of the skin, but obviously cannot remedy any other symptoms of too much sun that you might be suffering.

 CAUTION: Remember that everyone's skin is different. Please be aware that these tips do not replace the advice of your doctor or beauty professional and, although baking soda is mild and natural, particular care should still be taken with sensitive skin. When using any new product, it is advisable to do a patch test before using on large areas.

Deal with Chickenpox Spots

If you cast your mind back to your childhood illnesses, you may well remember how uncomfortable chickenpox was. There was the constant itching and the constant rebukes from your parents that you would scar yourself if you scratched the spots. Well, if you ever come into contact with some poor soul who is suffering from similar problems, suggest that they make a paste of baking soda and a little cool water. This can be applied directly to the spots without any fear of additional irritation. The paste will soothe the itching and make the patient feel much more comfortable.

Relieve Insect Bites and Stings

How annoying is it when those nasty little bugs creep up on you and give you such a bite that you feel as if a lion has mauled you? The worst ones are those mosquitoes, which you can only hear and not see. If you mix some baking soda into a paste with a little water and then smear it over the bite or sting, you will be amazed at how quickly it gives you relief from the itching or stinging.

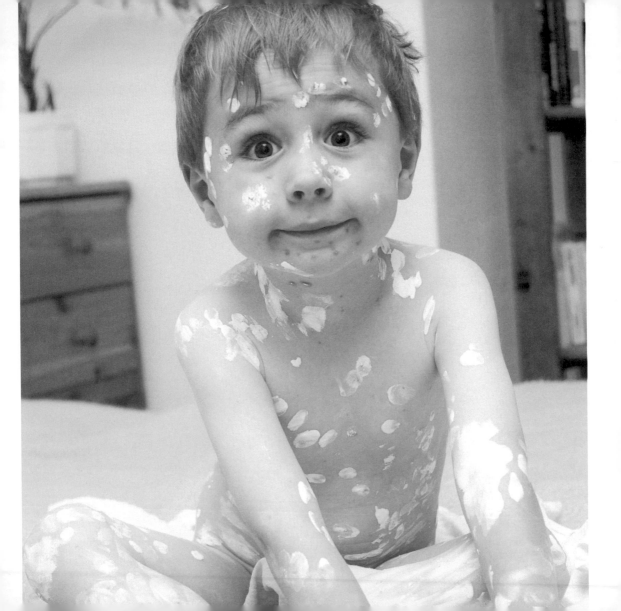

Help Acne

In a similar way to the relief of the itching of chickenpox spots, baking soda can be used to relieve acne, which can also be very itchy. The baking soda is again mixed with a little cool, but not cold, water into a paste. This should be applied to the affected area and left to dry for 5–10 minutes. The paste will relieve the irritation of the acne spots and will also act as an extremely mild and non-intrusive facial scrub. It will wash away easily from the face with cool water without damaging the skin in any way.

Ease Razor Burn

When we talk about razor burn, we automatically think of men shaving their face. But you can get razor burn on your legs or under your armpits too and that really can be just as uncomfortable for women as facial razor burn is for men. Once again, a baking soda paste can come to the rescue quite quickly. Make the paste quite a thin one and dab it on to the area affected by the razor burn to get almost immediate relief from the burning sensation.

However, if that does not work quite as quickly as you would like, then you could sprinkle neat baking soda on to the skin.

Exfoliate

Mixing a paste of three parts baking soda to one part water is a brilliant way of exfoliating the skin all over the body. It is also really inexpensive and easy to use.

The same quantities used for exfoliation can be mixed to a paste and applied to the face as a facial scrub. Use it after washing for that freshly scrubbed feeling. Apply the facial scrub in a circular movement to the face and then rinse it off with cool water.

Rough Patches

Those little parts of your body that seem to acquire hard skin for no particular reason, for example the elbows and knees, will definitely benefit from a baking soda paste. Mix to a paste and rub into the affected area to leave the skin feeling softer. It works on the soles and heels of the feet as well.

Pen Stains on Fingertips

You know when an ink, ballpoint or felt-tip pen decides to leak all over your fingers? Well, an easy way to remove this type of stain is to rub your hands together with a mix of baking soda and water. Rub away at the stain with confidence that it will not affect your skin but it will remove the stain. It will also remove some paint stains.

Hand Moisturizer

Remember the advertisement that went, 'Now hands that do dishes can feel soft as your face'? Well, that can be true of any washday red hands if you add a little baking soda into your

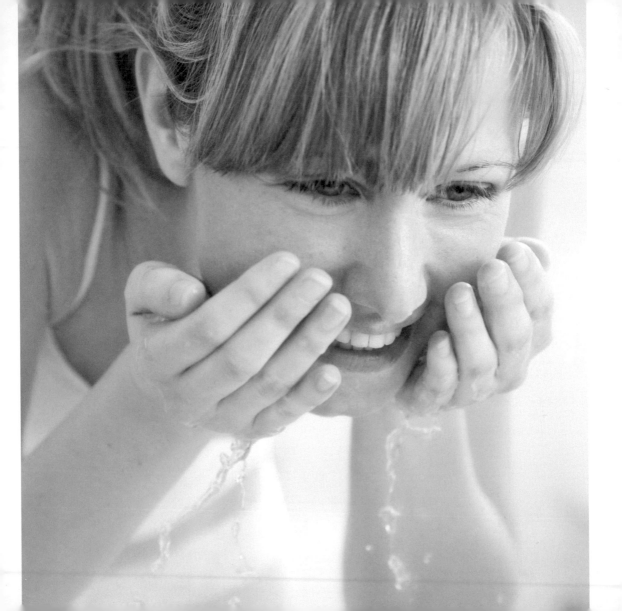

dishwater. The baking soda softens your hands, no matter how long you have to stand at the kitchen sink.

Baking Soda Bath Salts

Lying in a hot bath when your body is aching from exertion must be one of the nicest feelings. But you do not have to pay expensive prices to buy salts to add to the bath. Mix equal quantities of sea salt and baking soda (about 200 g/7 oz/1 cup is fine for one bath) and 250 ml/8 fl oz/1 cup of the shampoo of your choice while the water is running.

Once the bath is half-full, add your mixture and then top the bath up with more water. You will get some bubbles if you swirl your hand around and then you can soak to your heart's content.

Baking Soda Bath Oil

Making bath oil out of baking soda is just as easy as making bath salts, but this time you should let the bath fill completely before adding the mixture. Use the following ingredients and mix them in advance of your bath time.

In a mixing bowl, add 225 g/8 oz/1 cup sea salt, 4 tablespoons baking soda, 250 ml/8 fl oz/1 cup honey and 450 ml/16 fl oz/1¾ cups milk. Once the bath is full, pour the mixture in and add 115 ml/4 fl oz/½ cup of any of your favorite proprietary baby oil. This will give your skin a lovely soft and silky feel and you are sure to feel nicely relaxed too.

 CAUTION: Do not attempt to keep any baking soda bath oil over for the next bath – it has to be used fresh.

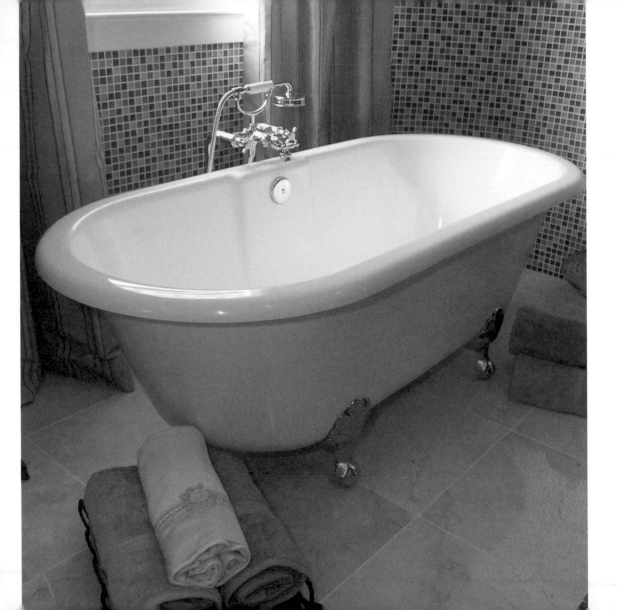

Dry Skin Bath Additive

If you are suffering with dry skin from the central heating or because of an allergy, you can relieve this by mixing 100 g/3½ oz/½ cup baking soda, 75 g/3 oz/1 cup oatmeal, 250 ml/ 8 fl oz/1 cup warm water and 1 tablespoon vanilla essence (or your favorite) into a paste. Let the mixture run under the faucet while you are running your bath. It certainly stops the itching.

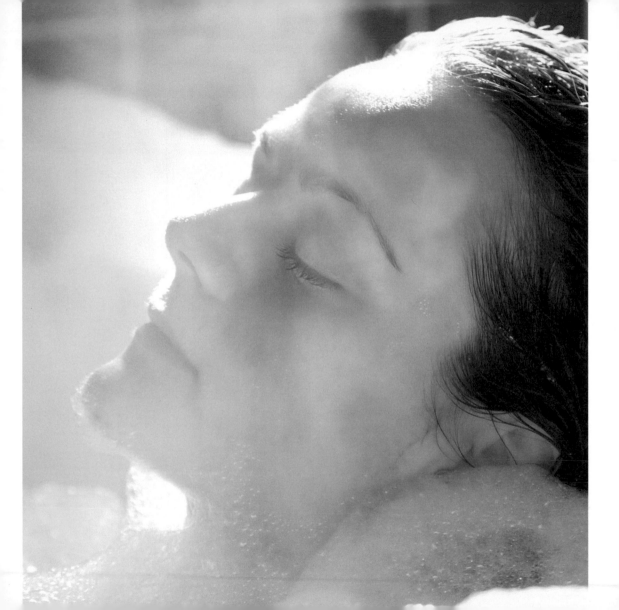

Hair

Conditioning the Hair

Sometimes, if you use the same shampoo or mousse all the time, you can get a build-up on your hair, making it feel lank, greasy, drab and lifeless. By adding 2 teaspoons baking soda to a teaspoon of your favorite shampoo and mixing them together, you can help to condition your hair and remove the build-up. You just have to wash and then rinse your hair as normal with your mixture. This mix gives your hair a good shine and leaves it feeling really clean.

Hairbrushes and Combs

How embarrassing is it when someone asks you if they can borrow one of your hairbrushes or combs and they look absolutely filthy, or even if they are visible when visitors appear at your home? Avoid this by boiling the dirt and grim away from your hairbrushes (if they are of a suitable material) for about 10 minutes in water and baking soda. Just add 200 g/ 7 oz/ 1 cup baking soda.

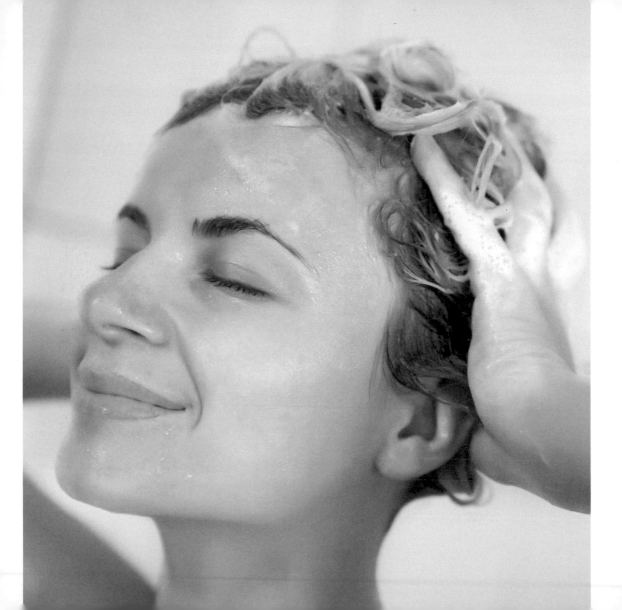

Teeth & Mouth

Whitening Teeth and Stain Removal

We all know that some of the proprietary brands of whitening toothpastes contain baking soda. But you can use a little baking soda once a week on your wet toothbrush to do much the same thing. Just dip your wet toothbrush into a little baking soda and brush your teeth as normal. The baking soda also helps remove any stubborn stains from your teeth. You should not swallow this paste and only use it if there are no signs of rawness on your gums.

For badly stained teeth, you could add a little hydrogen peroxide, although this should be used with care and definitely not swallowed.

Plaque Removal

We all know how quickly plaque and tartar build up on the teeth and how much better the teeth

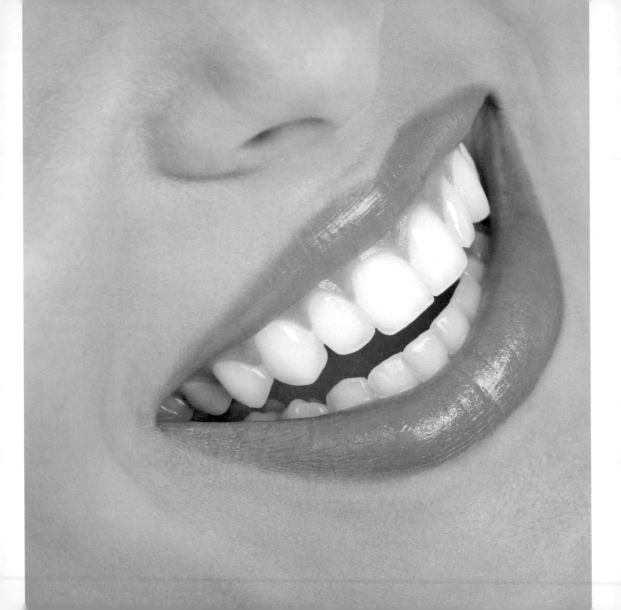

feel when the dentist has cleaned them. Using baking soda mixed with iodized salt on a wet toothbrush can help keep the plaque down.

Bespoke Toothpaste

If you like the taste of your regular toothpaste, then why not add some baking soda to it? By mixing the two together and placing the mixture into a sealed container, the mix will keep for ages. It will help keep down the plaque, as well as the stains, and keep your teeth whiter at the same time.

Cleaning Toothbrushes

We all do it – we grab the toothbrush without really giving any thought to the germs or bacteria that might be hiding on it. We brush away innocently. But the toothbrush can retain any number of germs and bacteria. To kill them, you can soak your toothbrush in a weak paste made of baking soda and water mixed together. The toothbrush would be fine soaking

all night and at least you would have peace of mind that it is clean when you come to use it the next morning.

Breath Freshener

You can make your own breath freshener – particularly useful if you dined on onions or garlic the night before! Using a gargle made of ½ teaspoon baking soda mixed with water could be part of your daily routine. This mix can kill off any germs and leave your mouth feeling much fresher.

Cleaning on the Move

Wherever you are, if you are expecting to get close or speak to people, it is always nice to feel confident that your mouth is fresh. If you are off to a meeting or a hot date, then dipping a piece of chewing gum into water and then into a small amount of baking soda can really help to make your mouth feel fresh and clean. It might be worth keeping a phial of it in your handbag or in the glove compartment of your car, just in case?

Nasty Cold Sores

Don't you just hate them? One minute you are just fine and then this huge, ugly and unsightly 'thing' appears on your lip. Don't panic though; you can treat a cold sore with some baking soda mixed with a little water. Gently – and we mean gently – rub the sore. You will feel relief and it will speed up the healing process.

 CAUTION: The cold sore virus can be carried on your toothbrush, so remember to soak it in baking soda too.

Retainers and Dentures

Braces, retainers and dentures can be soaked overnight in a mixture of baking soda and water. This mixture helps to kill off any germs that might have accumulated on them. It also helps to keep retainers looking bright and shiny. If dentures are badly stained, they can be scrubbed with a toothbrush that has been dipped in a soda paste.

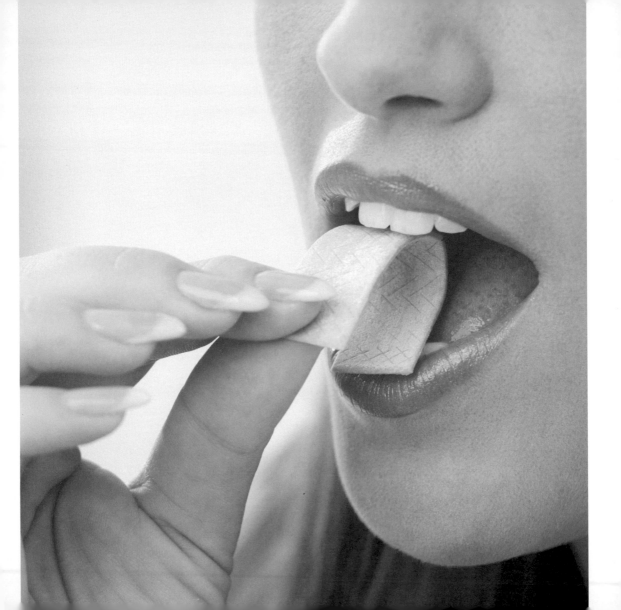

Odor & Feet

Smelly Feet

Smelly or itchy feet can really plague some people in the hot weather, but using baking soda as a talcum powder first thing in the morning can help keep the feet dry and itch-free all day. Use it before you put on your socks and footwear. Good for your feet and good for those around them too!

Underarm Deodorant

You can even use baking soda to make an underarm deodorant – how cool is that? Just mix together 4 teaspoons potassium alum (which you can buy in block form; it is used as an aftershave and rubbed over a freshly shaven face) with 2 teaspoons baking soda and 250 ml/8 fl oz/1 cup alcohol.

You can decant the mixture into a suitable plastic spray-capped bottle and it can be used daily. It keeps you fresh and dry all day long and the added bonus is that it does not contain any harmful chemicals.

Body Odor

Adding 100 g/3½ oz/½ cup baking soda to the bath water will help eliminate perspiration smells, as well as neutralizing acids and dispersing oil. If you use baking soda like

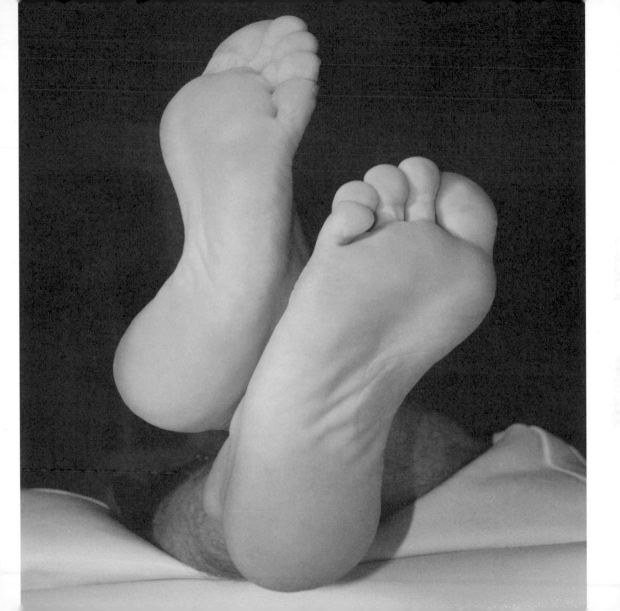

a talcum powder and apply it to your body with a powder puff, then you will feel fresh all day long. You can use it all over to keep the odors at bay.

Hands

You have just finished preparing a beautiful meal and the guests are due to arrive. You put your hands to your face, only to discover that they smell of garlic, onion and any combination of different food smells. Don't worry though; a little baking soda used as soap with a little water will quickly neutralize the smells and make you feel much better.

If your hands are particularly dirty, you can mix one measure of baking soda with three parts of either water or liquid hand wash to clean them up, then rinse off the grime. And don't forget to add some baking soda to the dishwater, too.

Talcum Powder

Baking soda straight from the pack works just like a talcum powder if you sprinkle it on to your skin. The baking soda helps absorb any excess moisture, particularly when the temperature is high, it is a bit too humid and you have been perspiring. Just like your favorite talcum powder, the baking soda makes you feel fresh all over.

Tired Feet

If you have been on your feet all day at work, or spent the day 'shopping till you nearly dropped', then a foot bath can feel wonderful. If you mix 200 g/7 oz/1 cup baking soda into some comfortably hot water, lower your feet gently in and then relax, you will be amazed how wonderful your feet feel afterwards. And your feet get softened too!

Baby Care

Because baking soda is not harmful to children or babies, it is

the perfect way to keep the nursery clean and fresh-smelling. Baking

soda can be used for many baby-related tasks. It can be used to clean

baby and his or her toys, as well as to eliminate those sometimes

overpowering baby smells around the home. You can use baking soda

with confidence around baby; it contains nothing that can

irritate the skin or cause any allergic reactions.

Bathing & Treatments

Baby Bath

Adding 200 g/7 oz/1 cup baking soda to baby's bath can help keep their skin wonderfully soft. You can use it instead of a bubble bath and rest easy that it will not irritate baby's skin.

Cleaning Bath Toys

Baby's bath toys can get a build-up of limescale. To remove this, sprinkle some baking soda on to a damp cloth and scrub clean. The baking soda also eliminates any lingering smells on the toys. For really stubborn limescale on the toys, you could make a paste of baking soda and water and scrub with an old toothbrush.

Cradle Cap Treatment

To effectively remove what can be unsightly cradle cap, mix together some baking soda and water. Smear it on to the affected area about an hour before bath time, then rinse the mixture off in the bath. Adding some baking soda to olive oil is another cradle cap treatment. Mix the two together and apply to the affected area by smearing it on.

 CAUTION: It is quite messy, so use old sheets if you can.

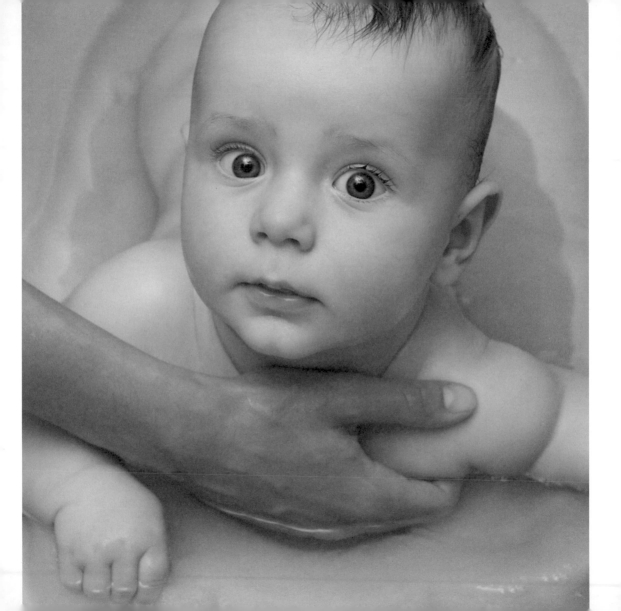

Diaper Rash Treatment

Diaper rash can be so uncomfortable for baby. If you have tried all the proprietary brands and they have not worked, try putting 1–2 teaspoons baking soda in the bath water after you've washed baby's face. The baking soda soothes baby's bottom and helps prevent diaper rash coming back.

If the diaper rash is causing serious discomfort, you can use baking soda at every diaper change. Dissolve 1 teaspoon in a cup of warm water and apply it to baby's bottom. Apply the mixture around the whole of the affected area and allow the mixture to air-dry naturally.

Thrush in the Mouth Treatment

If baby is suffering from thrush in the mouth, which is quite common in infants, mix together ¼ teaspoon baking soda, 250 ml/8 fl oz/1 cup water and a drop of liquid soap. Using a spotlessly clean cotton cloth, dab the mixture on to baby's tongue 4–6 times a day. It will not hurt baby.

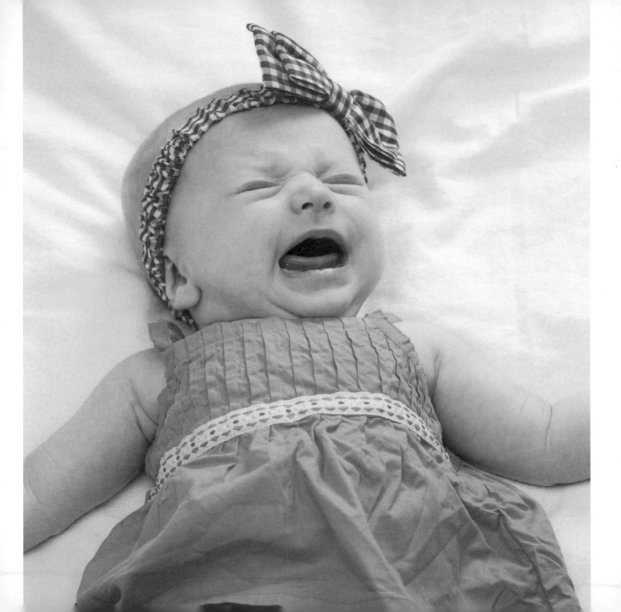

Cleaning & Odor Removal

Crib and Playpen

Because baking soda is not harmful to children or babies, it can be used to freshen up their room. It deodorizes smells and leaves the whole room smelling fresh.

Baby's crib can get quite grimy, particularly when they start pulling themselves up. To get rid of finger marks and grease, use a mixture of 100 g/3½ oz/½ cup baking soda, 50 ml/2 fl oz/¼ cup white vinegar and 2.25 l/4 pints/2¼ qts warm water. This mixture will get rid of smells in the crib too.

Any urine smells lingering in the nursery or child's room can be eliminated by sprinkling some baking soda on to the mattress of the crib or the bed when changing the sheets.

The playpen can get just as mucky, if not more so, than the crib – it often has lingering food, vomit and urine smells. Use the same mixture as for cleaning the crib. This will deodorize the playpen and make it a nicer place for baby to play.

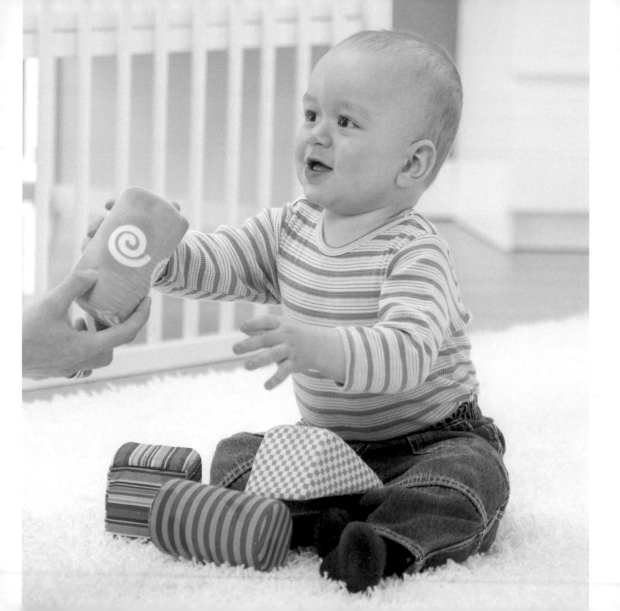

Bottles

Put a couple of tablespoons of baking soda in baby's bottles and fill them with water. Leave them overnight to soak and the sour smells will disappear.

If your baby's bottles can be put in the dishwasher, add some baking soda to the powder or tablet area. This will ensure that the dishwasher is clean enough to wash baby's bottles.

Teats and Pacifiers

When teats and pacifiers are not in use, they can be kept in cold water to which a pinch of baking soda has been added.

 CAUTION: Rinse well afterwards.

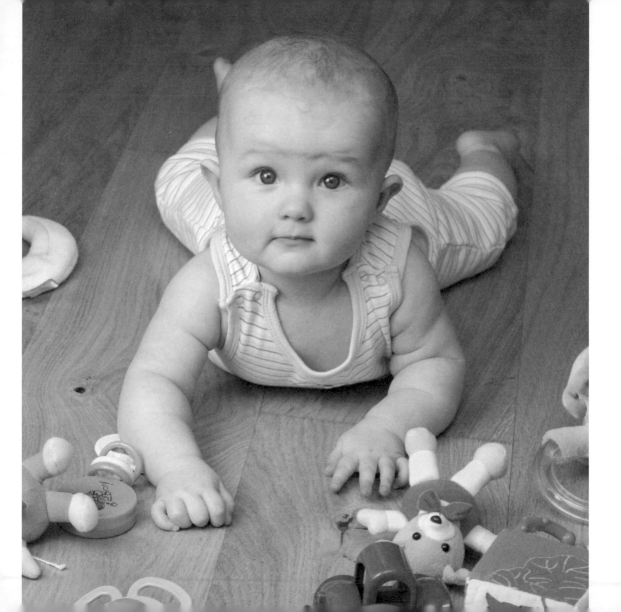

Teats and pacifiers can get discolored and stained, particularly when baby has moved on to solids. To remove the stains, mix a weak paste of baking soda and water, and give them a good scrub.

Toy Box

You can clean baby's toy box too. Once a month, mix together 200 g/7 oz/1 cup baking soda with an equal quantity of white vinegar. Use the mixture to clean the toy box and wipe all toys made of suitable material.

Cuddly Toys

Baking soda works on soft cuddly toys just as well. Put them in a clean pillowcase and add some baking soda, which you should sprinkle over the toys. If you give them a good shake they will come out smelling as fresh as daisies.

Crayon Marks

It is going to happen as your baby starts to get mobile – crayon on the walls and paintwork. Mix up a paste of baking soda and water. With an old toothbrush, apply the paste to the mark – magic, it's gone!

Washing Cloth Diapers

Some babies can get an allergy to washing powder that can cause diaper rash. Try putting 200 g/7 oz/1 cup baking soda in the wash to help avoid this.

The washing powder you use regularly can build up on diapers and baby clothes over time. To eliminate the build-up of the washing powder, replace it for one wash with 200 g/7 oz/1 cup baking soda. Use similar quantities to your washing powder. It won't lather so much but it will reduce the build-up.

You can keep your diapers looking bright and white if you add 100 g/3½ oz/½ cup baking soda to your washing machine. Put it in the powder chamber of your machine and you will be proud to hang those white diapers out to dry!

Diaper Bucket

If you use terry or cloth diapers, the bucket will inevitably get smelly. Sprinkle some baking soda (about 200 g/7 oz/1 cup) over each diaper as you add it to the bucket. This will deodorize the smells until washday.

Deodorizing Clothes

To eliminate baby smells from their clothes, and from your own, add 100 g/3½ oz/½ cup baking soda to water and soak the clothes for a few hours before washing.

If baby's clothes don't need a wash, but just need to be freshened up, you can sprinkle them with some baking soda to deodorize any lingering odors. Leave them overnight if you can and the stale smells will be gone by the morning.

Health

Baking soda is so safe to use that you can also ingest it.

Although it is artificially produced for mass use, it is a compound that also

occurs naturally as sedimentary mineral deposits; it is not the usual

horrible synthetic chemicals that we often wash down the drain, so it is not

harmful to us or to the environment as a whole. That's why it is so good

to use as a healthcare product. The other added advantage is that it is

cheap to buy and readily available in varying quantities.

Feel Better

Sports Drink

A really inexpensive and effective sports drink for all the family can be made by adding baking soda to a sugar-free children's drink. Mix 1 teaspoon baking soda, 1 tablespoon salt, 5 teaspoons sugar and 2.25 l/4 pints/2¼ qts water with the sugar-free drink and refrigerate it. It keeps for quite a while.

Your baking soda sports drink can be used in exactly the same way as any proprietary sports drink. Decant it into a reusable bottle and it can go anywhere with you or the children. It must be better for them than those fizzy, sugary drinks you can buy and it's cheaper!

Itchy Eyes

If you are suffering from itchy eyes, which could be the result of an allergy to pollen, you can soothe them with a baking soda eyewash. Add ½ teaspoon baking soda to half a glass of water and bathe the eyes with an eyebath. The mixture will keep in the fridge for a couple of days.

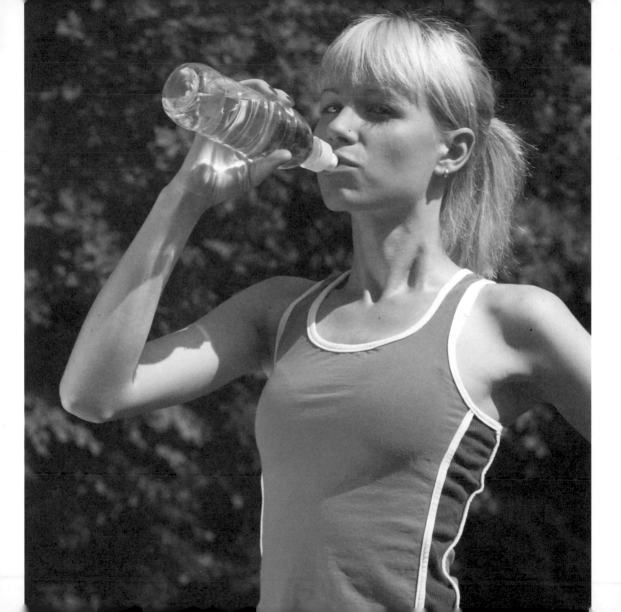

Contact Lenses

Daily-wear contact lenses need cleaning every day. Add a pinch of baking soda to your cleaner to make it mildly abrasive. This helps prevent build-up and could extend the life of the lenses.

Stuffy Nose

All bunged up? Using baking soda in a vaporizer can really help to clear a stuffy nose quickly. Fill the vaporizer with water to the indicated level, then add and stir in 1 teaspoon salt and 1 teaspoon baking soda until they are dissolved. Now breathe in the vapour to clear the congestion.

This is a really good tip for those who cannot or do not wish to use proprietary decongestants. Pregnant women, children and those who have medical conditions are often prevented from using medication. Baking soda is a safe alternative for everyone, whatever their circumstances.

Not only does baking soda in your vaporizer help clear your stuffy nose and reduce the symptoms of a cold, but it also deodorizes your house and removes lingering odors. How's that for good value?

Fever Reduction

If one of your loved ones has a high fever, there's nothing quite as effective and speedy to reduce the temperature as a baking soda. Add some baking soda to a cool, but not cold, bath and the temperature will plummet fast.

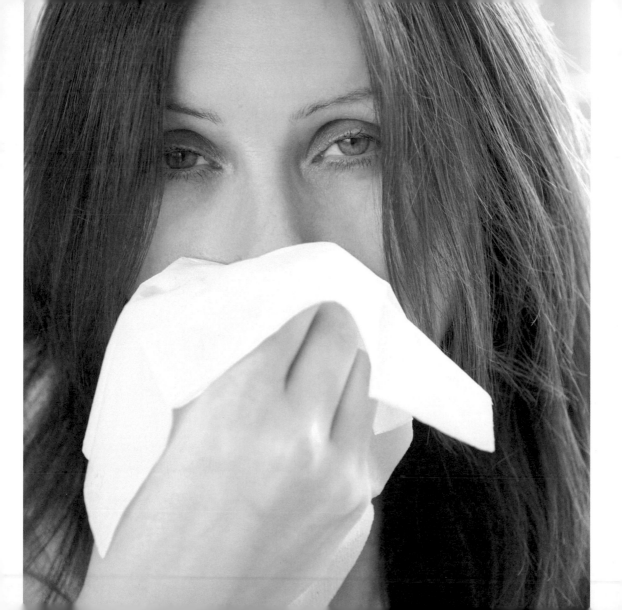

Children's high temperatures will really drop quickly if you pop them into the cool baking soda bath. They will feel much more comfortable. Of course, the added bonus is that it washes them squeaky clean at the same time as lowering their temperature.

Indigestion

Baking soda is known to be an effective antacid, so it can work for most stomach discomforts, particularly things such as indigestion and heartburn, which can make you feel really uncomfortable.

If you are one of those unfortunate people who regularly suffer from that bloated feeling after a meal, try sprinkling a little baking soda on to your food. It helps to reduce the build-up of gas that causes the bloated feeling. You can use baking soda whenever you have excessive bloating for whatever reason.

Some foods and drinks can give you heartburn every time you eat or drink them. But you don't have to suffer in silence or give up consuming them. Add 1 teaspoon baking soda to a glass of water and the burning feeling will disappear really quickly.

Other types of food, perhaps those that are greasy or really rich, can give you an upset stomach. This is particularly true if you make a habit of eating a good old english breakfast. When you do, try adding 1 teaspoon baking soda to your glass of water and the churning in the stomach soon settles down.

 CAUTION: Remember that the tips given here are not a substitute for a medical professional's assessment.

Outside & Maintenance

Yard & Do-It-Yourself

Probably the most fundamental reason for using baking

soda in the backyard, greenhouse and the outside of your house

is the cost. Baking soda is so cheap that needing large quantities of it to

complete the job is not a problem. In addition, because baking soda is a

natural product, the fact that you are using large amounts outside does not

pose a threat to the environment. There are so many useful

outside jobs you can do with it that you'll be amazed.

Tools & Equipment

Preserve those Tools

Shovels, forks, rakes – indeed all your gardening tools – should be put away for the winter in a clean state to help preserve them. You can make a thick paste with baking soda and white vinegar to give them a good clean. This will also stop rust forming over the winter months.

Polished Pots

If your garden pots are not frost-resistant, then they should also be stored away before winter sets in. But if you put them away dirty, you will find yourself faced with twice the job of cleaning them in the spring. Use the baking soda and white vinegar paste to clean them and then wash this off with some hot soapy water. They will sparkle in the spring!

Potato Trick

If any of your gardening tools have been neglected and become rusty, you can use a potato and some baking soda to renew them. Just peel the potato and keep dipping it in the baking soda and rub until the rust has all been removed from the metal tool. Shiny again!

Happy Pots

If you line your terracotta pots with a thin layer of baking soda before adding the soil, it will help to keep the soil fresh. It will kill any lingering bacteria and germs from previous plants.

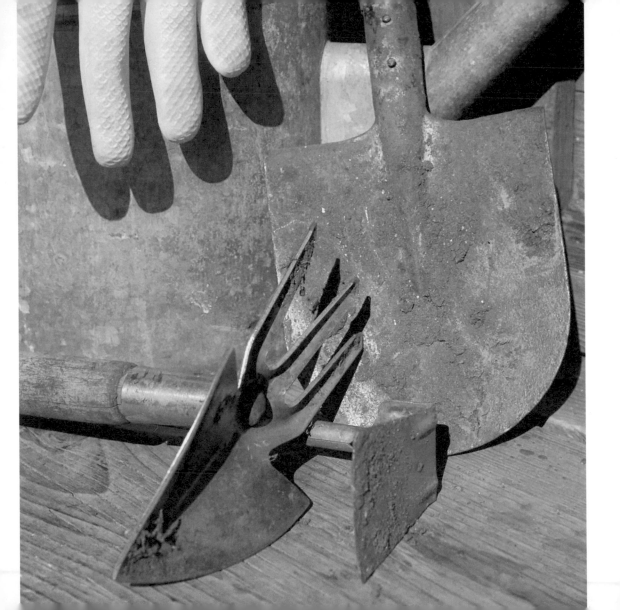

Outdoor Furniture & Surfaces

Wash that Plastic

Backyard furniture can be expensive, so if you want to prolong its life, you have to take care of it. Plastic furniture should be washed before it is put into storage for the winter. Add 200 g/7 oz/1 cup baking soda to some hot soapy water and wash the furniture with the mix. This will help remove stains too.

Bright Whites

If your backyard furniture is all white in color, you can keep it that way by adding some lemon juice to your baking soda mix. Squeeze the lemon juice into your hot water and baking soda mix. It is as good as bleaching the white furniture.

Clean the Grill

Cleaning the barbecue grill can be a tiresome job and quite a messy one. To clean the appliance without causing any scratching to the stainless steel surface, try sprinkling some baking soda straight on to a damp brush. Coat the grill well with the baking soda, give it a good scrub, then rinse clean.

Pool Perfection

Whilst you are busy cleaning the backyard in general, the children's paddling pool might benefit from a bit of tender loving care too. Get rid of any mould or mildew by rubbing it inside and out with a mix of water, baking soda and white vinegar. Good as new and safe for the children next year.

Walkways, Patios and Decking

Although it might take a whole box of baking soda to clean your walkways and patio areas, it is still effective and inexpensive. Wet the baking soda a little bit after you've sprinkled it over your concrete areas and then scrub with a stiff broom to remove stains and moss from the concrete.

You could use the sprinkling and brushing technique for cleaning your wooden decking too. Sprinkle the baking soda on and brush with a dry broom, but wash away the dirt and grime with water afterwards.

Birdbaths

Even the birdbath needs a good clean from time to time, but don't worry about harming the creatures that drink from it or bathe in it. Using baking soda and water mixed to a paste will remove all stubborn grime and will not affect the birds at all.

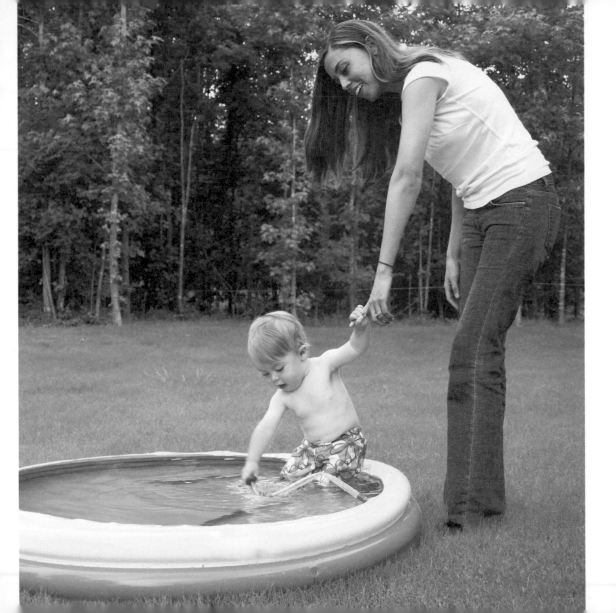

Hygienic Hammocks

Backyard hammocks can be wiped down with a baking soda and water mix. This will get rid of any built-up grime and also bring out their color, not to mention making them smell really fresh for you too when you swing next summer.

Cleaner and Safer Toys

Children's backyard toys, such as trampolines or slides and seesaws, as well as plastic cars and scooters, all need the baking soda touch. Baking soda mixed with water will bring the colors back to life and keep the dust levels at a minimum. It must be better and healthier for the children to use clean toys in the backyard?

Plastic backyard toys can become brittle if they are stored away in a warm environment during the winter months. To counteract this effect, you can wipe the toys with a mixture of baking soda and white vinegar. The two ingredients when mixed together will clean and protect the toys at the same time.

Snow and Ice

Baking soda acts very much like salt on snow and ice. Because the baking soda, like salt, freezes at a lower temperature than water, it is an ideal way to melt snow once it has lain on your concrete. Sprinkle it over freshly fallen snow to help it melt quickly, then add some more in case the slush freezes. For a more preventative measure, if snow and ice are forecast, you can stop the water from freezing overnight by sprinkling baking soda on to your concrete. Use it on your pathways and steps in the backyard to stop falls and accidents. Sprinkle it generously and cover as much of the concrete as you can.

Greenhouses & Plants

Wash Down

Some people use a store-bought cleaner to clean their greenhouses in the fall. However, if you want an ingredient that is just as effective, but cheaper, you can use baking soda. Wash all the surfaces, including the roof and walls, with baking soda and water. It will kill any mould and bacteria that may have formed during the growing season, as well as making the glass shine.

For an alternative mixture to wipe down the surfaces in your greenhouse and remove dirt and grime, mix 4 teaspoons baking soda with 120 ml/4 fl oz/½ cup white vinegar and 2.25 l/4 pts/2¼ qts water. You can even put this mixture into a spray bottle, bit by bit, to make it easier to apply. Simply wipe off the dirt with a damp cloth.

Greenhouse Fungicide

Baking soda has been used for years as a mild fungicide, particularly by organic growers. It can be used against powdery mildew and other plant diseases in the greenhouse too. Mix 5 tablespoons baking soda with 4 l/7 pts/4 qts water and spray the greenhouse and the affected plants.

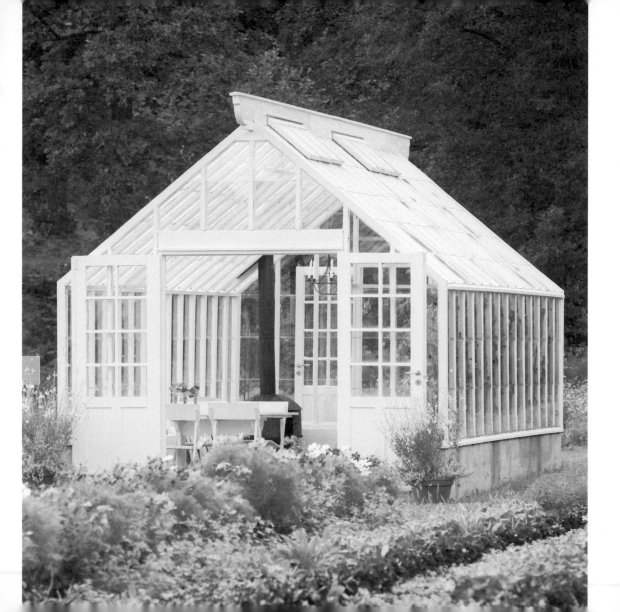

Routine for Roses

No matter how careful a gardener you are, mould and mildew still spread really quickly once they take hold. To keep mould on plants, particularly roses, at bay, you can spray with a mixture of 200 g/7 oz/1 cup baking soda and 2.25 l/4 pts/2¼ qts water. It really stops the mould from spreading to other plants.

Clean the Bottle

When you have sprayed your garden plants, be sure to kill any mildew or fungus inside the spray nozzle. Add a little baking soda and this should do the job for you. Also, before you put

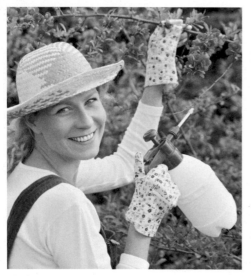

your sprayer into storage, do the same thing so it's fresh when watering time comes around again.

Defeat Disease

You can mix 4 teaspoons baking soda into 7.5 l/11¾ pts/7½ qts water to treat diseased plants. Apply the mixture generously to the diseased plants with a hand-held spray.

✋ **CAUTION:** You will have to fill the spray several times, but do make sure you cover all the diseased parts of the plant, including the foliage.

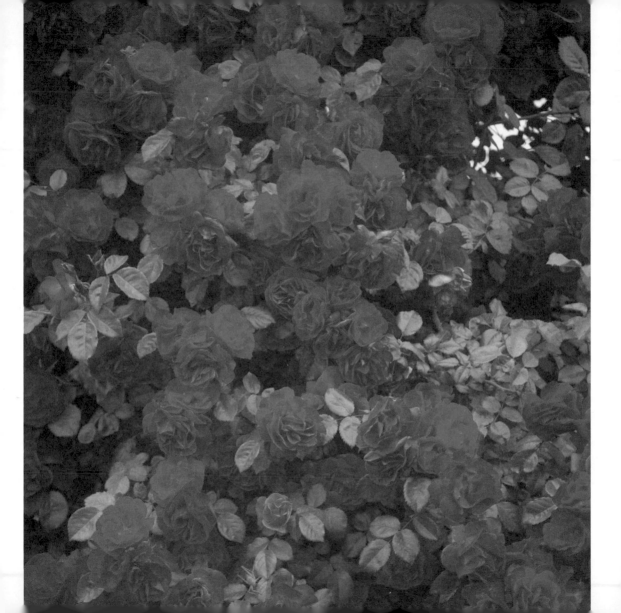

Free the Lawn from Mould

If your lawn needs some serious attention, there is no better way to give it a boost than baking soda, particularly if you have problems with mould. Use 1 tablespoon to 4 l/ 7 pts/4 qts water and spray the lawn, or you can apply it with a watering can. It kills off mould or mildew without having to use a fungicide and gives the lawn a bit of a tonic.

Another way of applying the soda is to fill a sock or an old pair of tights with some neat baking soda. Beat the side of the sock or tights with your hands to release the powder. You get more of an even spread this way and you can always water it in with a hose if it doesn't rain.

Acid or Alkaline?

You can test the acidity of your backyard soil by adding a pinch of baking soda to 1 tablespoon of your soil. If the mixture fizzes, the soil's pH is probably low and could do with a weak solution of baking soda and water. This mixture will help plants such as geraniums, begonias and hydrangeas to bloom. They like a more alkaline soil.

Sweeter Tomatoes

Tomato plants like baking soda too! Sprinkle a little around their roots regularly from the first planting. This will reduce their acidity and make them even sweeter to eat.

Blooming Marvellous

After cutting flowers from the garden to take into the house, why not try dipping their stems in a mild soda and water mix? It will help the flowers to stay fresh longer and kills any bacteria.

Pest Control

Ants No More!

Ants – whoever needs them? Although they don't do much damage, they are still off-putting, particularly if they are near your doors and windows. You can sprinkle neat baking soda around their entrance and exit areas to help get rid of them and hopefully stop them getting into the house.

Ants also seem to love children's sandpits. If they are invading your child's sandpit, then mix a whole box of baking soda into the sand. That should keep them away!

Fleeing Fleas

Fleas are not fans of baking soda either. You can sprinkle it on your lawn, where they often congregate, believe it or not, or you can sprinkle the baking soda directly on to your pet to make sure they don't stay on too long.

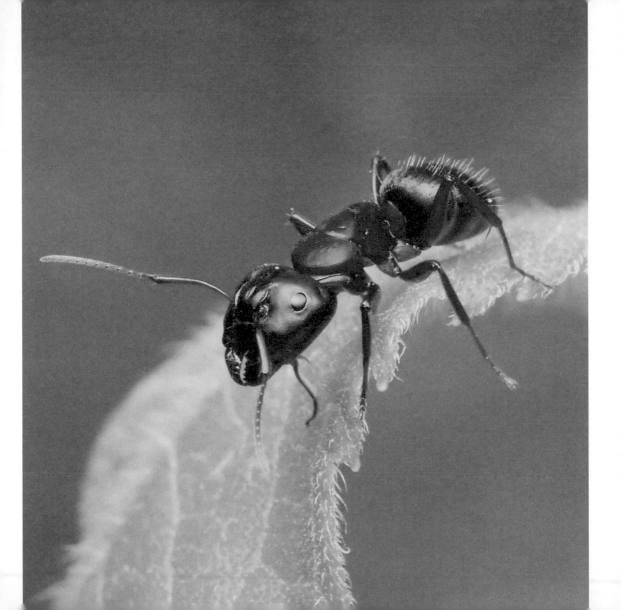

Clear out Cockroaches

Cockroaches seem to like damp places and places where water congregates. You do not want cockroaches in your home because they spread so many germs. Try to keep damp areas free of the little devils, particularly around water pipes and in cellars, by sprinkling neat baking soda in these areas.

Repel Rabbits

No matter how sweet we think they are, rabbits can do a lot of damage in the backyard. They can be particularly harmful to plants that have been recently planted and especially to lettuces and cabbages. To ward off rabbits, sprinkle some baking soda generously around the vegetable patch.

Say No to Slugs and Snails

Slugs and snails can do even more damage than rabbits. They can destroy a newly planted vegetable or bedding plant overnight by eating the sweet leaves. At least if you use the baking soda generously, you should be able to deter most of these pests in one fell swoop, and your plants might actually feed you.

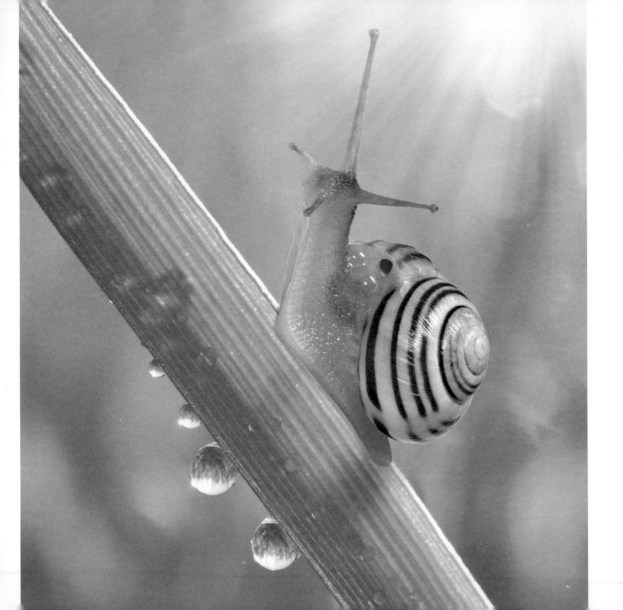

Painting & Decorating

Soften Paintbrushes

If you have been really bad and not cleaned your paintbrushes properly the last time you used them, there is an overnight remedy. Mix together 200 g/7 oz/1 cup baking soda, 50 g/2 oz/¼ cup white vinegar and 2.25 l/4 pts/2¾ qts hot water. Soak the brushes in the mixture overnight and by morning they should be soft and ready to use again.

Sticky Residue Remover

When you have painted a window, to remove any glue left from masking tape, simply make a paste of baking soda and water. Rub gently with the paste to remove the glue residue.

You can use the same mix of baking soda and water to remove poster glue from windows. If you have been advertising a local event and there is some glue residue on the window, use this mix to remove it completely and easily.

Wash Down Walls

To keep your outside walls clean and bright, you can wash them down with a mixture of 100 g/3½ oz/ ½ cup baking soda to each 4 l/7 pts/4 qts water. It will clean efficiently and bring colors back to almost new. The mix can be used on most outside wall materials.

You can use the same mixture (100 g/3½ oz/½ cup baking soda to each 4 l/7 pts/4 qts water) to wash down your walls and paintwork before you begin to repaint them. This will remove all the dirt and grime, as well as any of the old paint that may be flaking.

Stripping Wallpaper

If you are planning to strip wallpaper, you can make the job much easier if you add 1 tablespoon baking soda to the water. Stir it in until it has dissolved and then wet the walls ready for stripping in the normal way. Let it soak in well and you will be amazed how much more easily the paper comes off.

Vehicles

Cars, bikes and motorbikes can be messy. Let's face it, we spend so much time in our vehicles that it is not surprising that sometimes they are our pride and joy and at others they are the bane of our lives. If we are not worrying about cleaning them then we are worrying about selling them. Keeping them in tiptop condition can only be good when it comes to getting a good price for 'her'. Being safe when we are working on our cars and bikes is so vitally important. Baking soda can help with all these things.

Cars & Bikes

Oil and Gas Spills

If you have a car that leaks oil or gas on the floor of your garage, then you might like to try the baking soda remedy for removing the stain. You just need to sprinkle a mixture of baking soda and salt over the spill. Leave it for a while to soak up all the oil or gas, then all you need to do is sweep the floor. Even if the oil or gas leaks on to your driveway, baking soda and salt will still lift the stain efficiently.

 CAUTION: Give the mix plenty of time to soak up all the liquid up before you sweep the driveway.

Odor Removal

If the car has not been used for some time, it can begin to smell musty inside. Neutralize these smells by sprinkling baking soda all over. You can put it in the boot, on the seats and on the mats without any fear of damaging the interior upholstery.

Extinguishing Fires

Small fires can be extinguished in a garage or workshop using baking soda. Pour a complete box of the baking soda on to the fire and it will extinguish it. It is a good idea to keep some on the shelf just in case, particularly if you regularly use a naked flame in the garage or workshop.

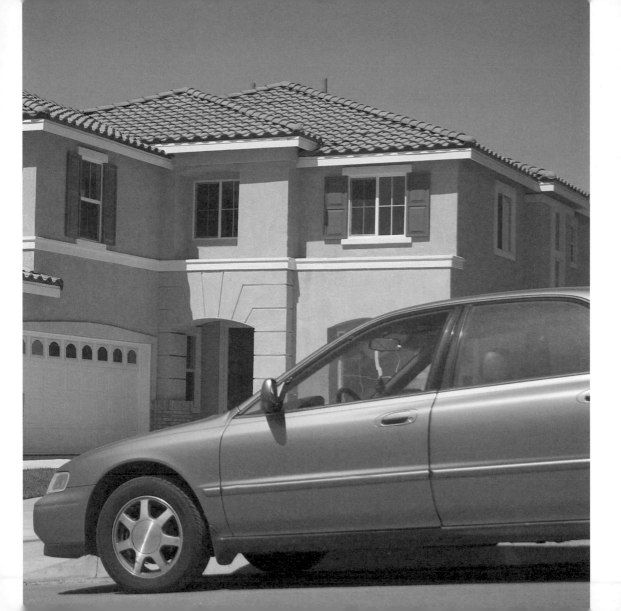

You could also keep some baking soda in the boot of your car. It is particularly effective at extinguishing electrical fires. The baking soda smothers the fire and brings its temperature down quite quickly.

 CAUTION: Baking soda should not be applied to fires in deep fryers as it may cause the grease to splatter.

Bugs on Bikes

To remove bugs that may have got stuck to the windows or wing mirrors of your car or motorbike, you can wash them with a mixture of baking soda and water. The bugs will come off quite easily, but you won't scratch the glass.

Rusty Bikes

Bicycles can go rusty quite quickly, particularly if they are housed in a garage or shed. Vinegar and baking soda mixed to a paste will give them a general clean, but if there are any rust patches developing, give them a particularly good scrub. The mix should remove the rust quite easily.

Soda Shine

To give the chrome on a bicycle or motorbike an extra shine, apply a baking soda and water paste. Smear it on to the chrome and then leave it to dry naturally in the air. When it is dry, you can buff the chrome with a soft cloth and you will be able to see your face in it.

Kids' Stuff

Fun Projects for Children

What a really fun and inexpensive play ingredient baking soda can be. Your children will be safely amused for hours making clay, volcanoes and rockets out of baking soda. The ingredients are all cheap and easy to get hold of and the added bonus is that there is nothing that can harm the children. What more could a busy parent ask, particularly when the children are also learning useful science- and maths-related stuff at the same time?

Clay

Your children will love making this easy-to-mould clay. It is safe to use and the ingredients are so cheap – certainly much less than most proprietary brands of clay. The children can add food coloring to it if they wish at the very beginning of the project, or they can also decorate it with paint, felt-tip pens or watercolor pens after they have formed their shapes. This recipe makes a good-sized piece of baking soda clay.

You Will Need:

1 large box (400 g/14 oz/2 cups) baking soda
200 g/7 oz/1 cup cornstarch
250 ml/8 fl oz/1 cup water
1 tbsp vegetable oil

1   Place all the ingredients into an old saucepan. You can add the food coloring of your children's choice at this stage, or you can wait and color at the end.

2   Heat the mixture very slowly, stirring all the time, until the mixture becomes thick and uniform in shape. The heating stage usually takes about 15 minutes or so on a low heat.

3   When the mixture is the right consistency, pour it out of the saucepan and on to an old plate.

4   Cover the clay with a damp cloth and leave it to cool for about an hour.

5   Once the clay has cooled enough to be handled, you can sprinkle some more cornstarch on to a wooden board and knead the clay, as you would bread, until the clay is smooth.

6   Now you can let the children loose. The clay can be moulded into any shape that your children wish. They can also use their favorite colors to highlight the shapes. Felt-tip pens or watercolor pens are good for this important task.

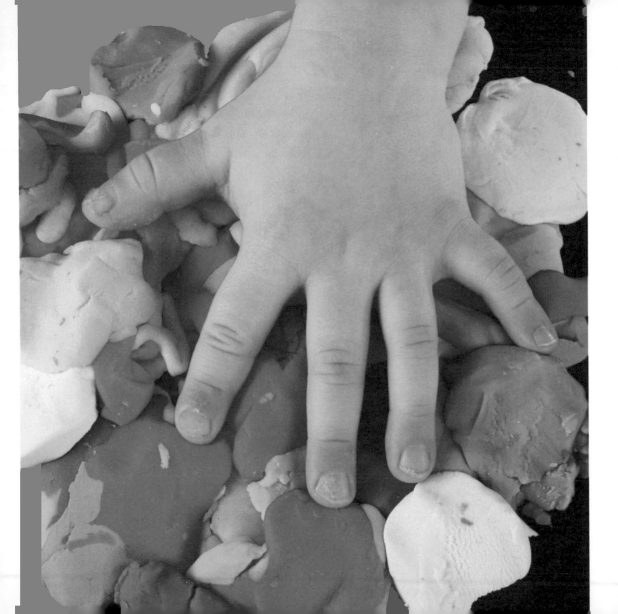

Fizzy Sherbet

There is no cooking involved in making this fun fizzy treat for the children, but getting the taste right can be a case of trial and error. The sugar or citirc acid may have to be adjusted to give the right level of sweetness or tartness, which varies from person to person.

This is a really good science-related project. Children will learn that the sugar and the citric acid give the sherbet the flavor, and that the carbon dioxide produced when the citric acid and baking soda mix together with their saliva gives the fizzing action on the tongue.

Start With:

2 tsp superfine sugar or confectioners' sugar; 1 tsp powdered citric acid; ½ tsp baking soda

1   Mix the ingredients together.
2   Test for sweetness and if necessary add some more sugar.
3   If the sherbet does not taste quite lemony enough, add some more citric acid.
4   If the sherbet isn't quite fizzy enough on your tongue, then add some more baking soda.

You can also vary the flavor of your sherbet when you have this initial ingredient mix just right. But remember that all the ingredients have to be dry, otherwise the sherbet will fizz with any liquid you add before it gets on to your tongue. You could try adding vanilla, coffee, cloves, cinnamon, dry ginger and a host of other dry ingredients.

You can simply spoon the sherbet into your mouth with a spoon or shovel-shaped straw – but it is particularly enjoyable for children to dip a lollipop or stick of liquorice into the sherbet.

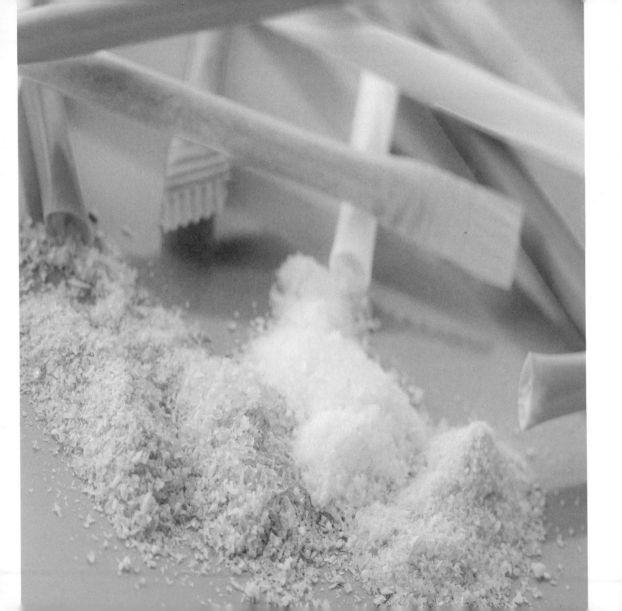

Crunchy Toffee

Crunchy toffee, also known by some as 'cinder toffee', is a really fun project to make with the children. It is also good to eat as a special treat. Honeycomb toffee is a flexible recipe, which means you can add ingredients to it to bring about any number of changes in taste.

You Will Need:

a little butter; 1 tsp baking soda; 150 g/5 oz/¾ cup sugar; 4 tbsp honey or corn syrup

1 Lightly grease a baking tray with butter. Melt together the sugar and the honey or corn syrup over a low heat, stirring continuously to prevent burning, until they have caramelized.
2 Slowly add the baking soda. Keep stirring continuously to prevent burning. As the baking soda hits the hot caramel, it will bubble up quickly and turn a burnt orange color.
3 Once the mixture has stopped rising because of the baking soda, you can carefully remove it from the heat.
4 Pour the toffee mix on to the greased baking tray and cover with clingfilm/plastic wrap.
5 Once the toffee mix has cooled sufficiently, place in the fridge to harden.
6 Cut the crunchy toffee into bite-size squares to serve.

 CAUTION: Do not leave young children unattended around hot appliances.

Variations

Children's favorite flavorings, such as orange or strawberry, can be added at the same time as the baking soda. Alternatively, or in addition, you can dip the squares of toffee into melted chocolate and leave to set. You can even sprinkle chopped nuts on top of the still-wet chocolate.

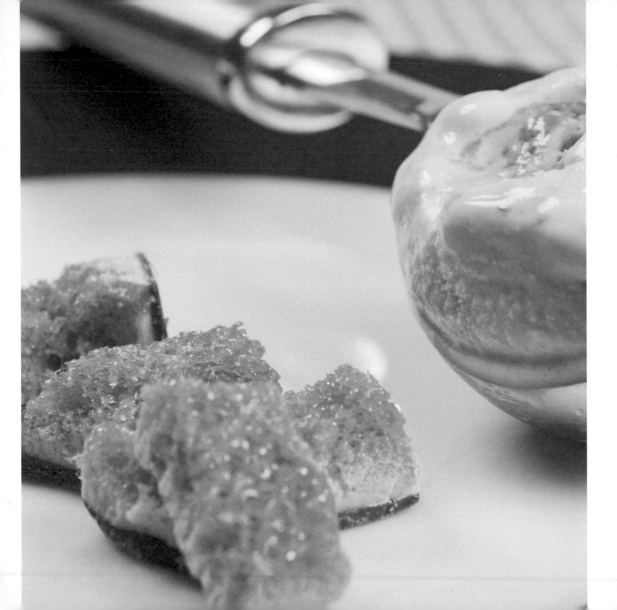

Inflate a Balloon

Showing children how to inflate a balloon using baking soda and vinegar is a really good science-related activity. The project gives them the chance to learn much about chemical reactions and the nature of solids, liquids and gases.

When the baking soda and the vinegar you use in this activity are mixed together in your plastic bottle, they form carbon dioxide. As the carbon dioxide gas is made, pressure builds up inside the bottle so that the gas produced escapes into the balloon and inflates it.

You Will Need:

2 heaped tsp baking soda; 150 ml/5 fl oz/⅗ cup vinegar;
plastic drink bottle that can hold 600 ml/1 pt/2½ cups; balloon; plastic funnel

1   Insert your plastic funnel into the neck of the balloon.
2   Spoon into the funnel your 2 heaped teaspoonfuls baking soda. Shake
     the baking soda so that it filters through the funnel and into the balloon.
3   Next, you need to pour your vinegar into the bottle, again using your plastic funnel.
4   Whilst holding the balloon tightly so that none of the baking soda falls out,
     you can now stretch the neck of the balloon over the neck of the plastic bottle.
5   Tip the balloon so that the baking soda falls into the vinegar and the two mix.

As the chemicals in the vinegar and the baking soda mix in the bottle and give off fumes, your balloon will begin to inflate. Once the balloon has stopped inflating, you can remove it from the bottle and tie the balloon in a knot.

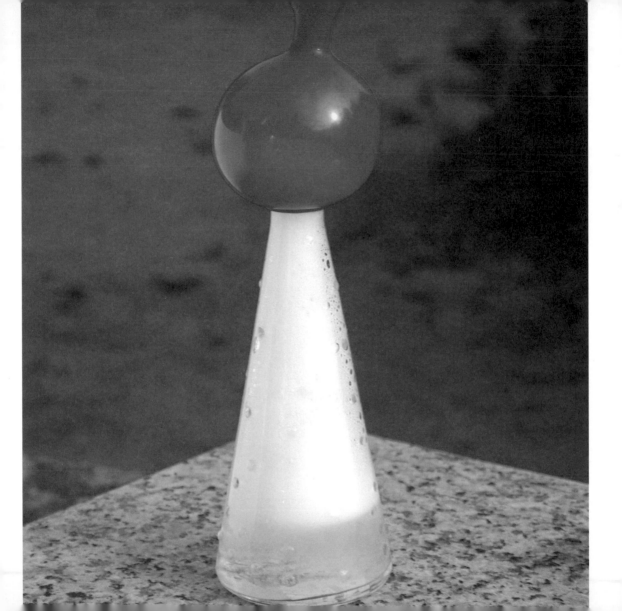

Volcanic Eruption

This inexpensive project is a craft and science project. It takes time to organize, but is worth the effort; the kids will love it.

To Make the 'Volcano' Dough:

700 g/1½ lb/6 cups flour
350 g/12 oz/2 cups salt
4 tbsp vegetable oil
500 ml/18 fl oz/2 cups water

1   In a large bowl, mix all the dry ingredients together.
2   Add half the water and oil and knead to form a dough-like consistency.
3   Add the remaining water and oil gradually, working into a smooth and firm dough. If the mixture feels too dry, add more water.

To Create the Volcano:

plastic bottle that can hold 2 l/3½ pts/2 qts
2 heaped tsp baking soda
150 ml/5 fl oz/⅔ cup vinegar
2 l/3½ pts/2 qts warm water (continued overleaf)

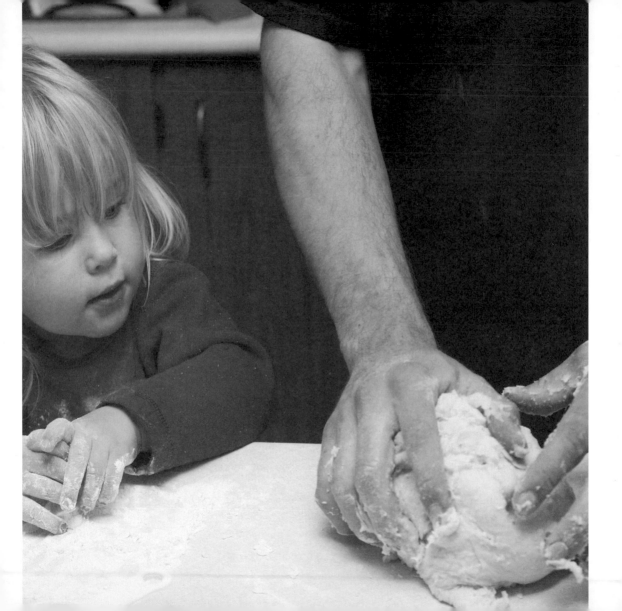

few drops food coloring
few drops liquid soap
2 tbsp baking soda
baking tray

1   Stand the clean, dry plastic bottle on your baking tray and shape the dough around the bottle to form a volcano shape. Avoid dropping dough inside the bottle and leave the bottle opening free.

If time allows, let the volcano dry for 2 or 3 days before going any further. You could paint it, providing the bottle opening and the inside of the bottle remain dry. However, if you cannot wait to see the full effect of the volcano, you can make the lava straightaway:

2   Put a few drops of your chosen food coloring into the bottle.
3   Pour over the warm water until you have almost filled the bottle.
4   Add a few drops of liquid soap into the bottle.
5   Then add the baking soda to the soapy water in the bottle.
6   Now to make the lava explode! Just pour in your vinegar.

When the baking soda and vinegar mix together, they produce carbon dioxide gas. This bubbles up and forces your colored lava to erupt.

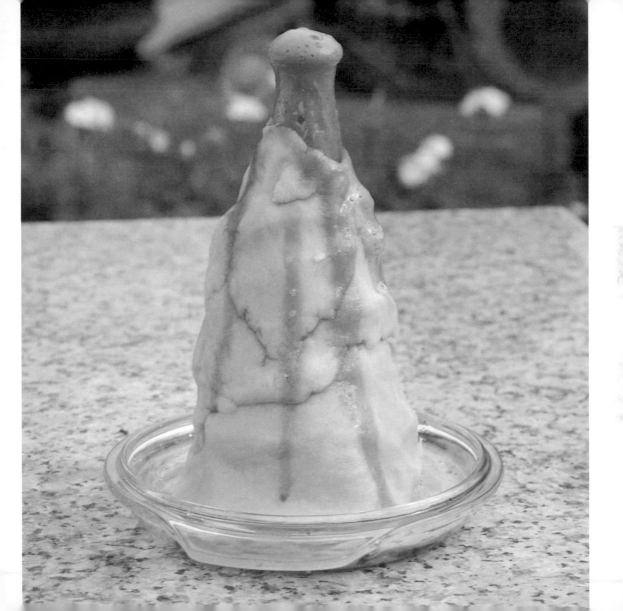

Mini Rocket

The children will really enjoy this exciting and creative project.

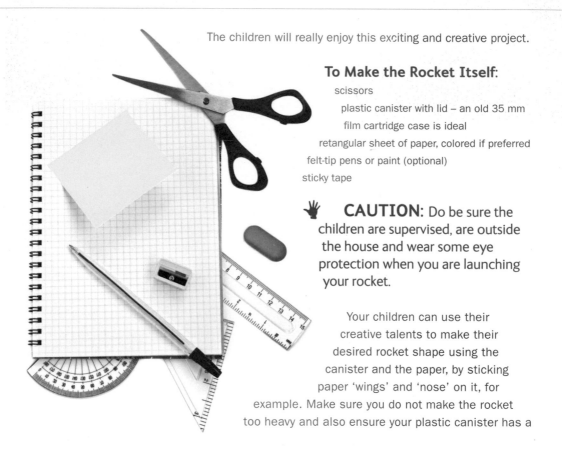

To Make the Rocket Itself:

scissors

plastic canister with lid – an old 35 mm film cartridge case is ideal

retangular sheet of paper, colored if preferred

felt-tip pens or paint (optional)

sticky tape

CAUTION: Do be sure the children are supervised, are outside the house and wear some eye protection when you are launching your rocket.

Your children can use their creative talents to make their desired rocket shape using the canister and the paper, by sticking paper 'wings' and 'nose' on it, for example. Make sure you do not make the rocket too heavy and also ensure your plastic canister has a

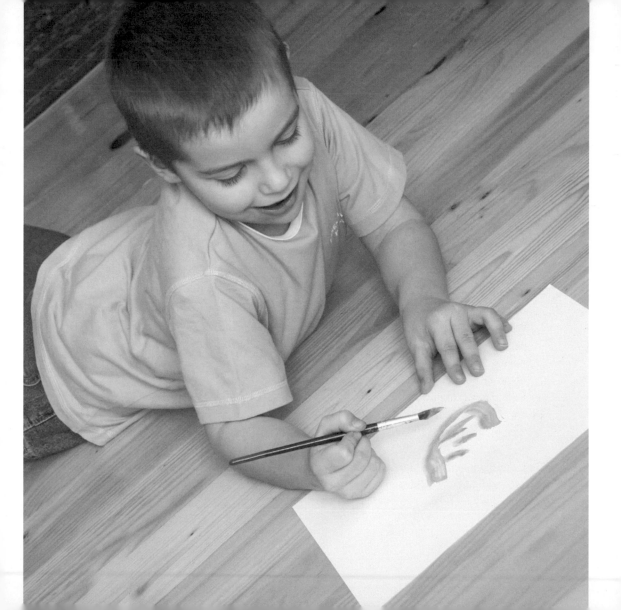

removable lid. You can make the rocket well in advance of launching it, particularly if the children want to paint or color their rocket. When you are ready to launch the rocket, it's time to make the rocket fuel.

To Make the Fuel:

½ tsp baking soda
½ tsp vinegar
tissue

You should not allow your baking soda and vinegar to mix until you are ready to launch the rocket. But when you are ready, you can:

1 Wrap your baking soda in a tissue. Make a parcel that will easily fit inside the lid of your plastic canister.
2 Fix the baking soda parcel into the lid of the plastic canister with a little sticky tape. Alternatively, make a paste with the baking soda and a little water and pack this into the lid.
3 Pour the vinegar into your plastic canister.
4 Carefully put the lid on to the canister, then turn the canister upside down so that the vinegar soaks through the tissue paper and mixes with the baking soda.

When the baking soda and the vinegar combine, they will make carbon dioxide gas. This gas will force the plastic canister to pop off the lid. The rocket will launch into the air, so stand back and enjoy!

Food

Culinary Tips

In addition to using baking soda in recipes, baking soda can also be used in a number of ways to prepare foodstuffs ready for cooking, or to preserve them for future use. Baking soda is a really useful and practical addition to any cupboard shelf. It is cheap and, because it is not harmful to our bodies, you can use it to your heart's content. Baking soda is so versatile that it is amazing it does not carry a huge price tag.

Meat & Poultry

Free of Feathers

Sometimes, when you buy a chicken, there are a few feathers left on the skin. They won't do you any harm, but they can be a bit off-putting. To get rid of these quickly and easily, just rub the skin of the chicken with baking soda. Rinse the baking soda off before cooking the bird.

Tender Fowl

Baking soda is also really good for tenderizing chicken meat. Rub the meat liberally with some baking soda and then rinse it thoroughly for a really tender chicken.

Crispy Chicken

If you want the chicken skin to be crispy, you can rub in some baking soda before cooking. Crispy skin and tender meat – delicious!

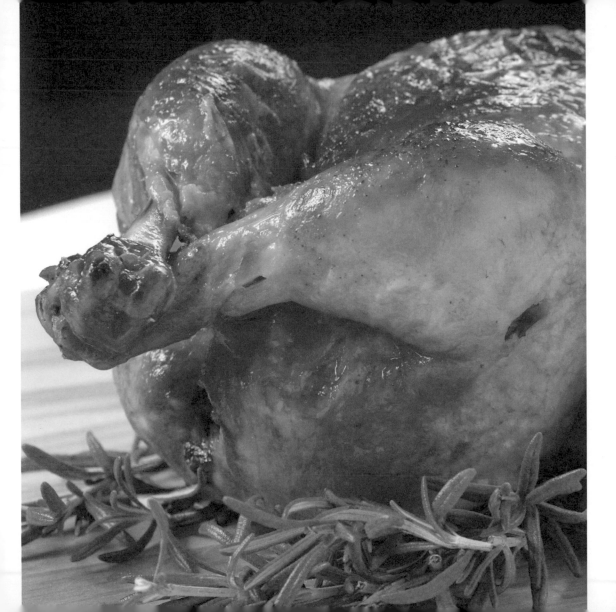

Tone Down Flavor

You can use baking soda to reduce the strong flavor of meats such as venison, particularly if you are planning to preserve the meat. Add the baking soda to your preserving jar to get rid of an overwhelming flavor.

No Fowl Smell

If you are plucking and preparing your own chicken, you can get rid of the sometimes strong smell by sprinkling some baking soda into the cavity before drawing out the giblets.

Pork Crackling

If you like your pork crackling really crisp, then baking soda can do this for you. Sprinkle and smear some baking soda on to the pork skin before cooking. The baking soda will help the skin to really crisp up for you. Score the skin as usual, with crisscross cuts using a sharp knife. Cutting like this helps to crisp up the skin too and makes it easier to cut and share, because everyone will want some!

Smearing baking soda on to the skin of your pork meat will not only give you a crispy crackling, but it will also help keep the meat tender.

Marinade Me Tender

You can add ½ teaspoon baking soda to your meat marinade prior to cooking stir-fry dishes. The baking soda will help soften the texture of the meat, particularly if the meat you have bought is one of the tougher cuts. The meat will melt in your mouth.

Vegetables

Vibrant Carrots

Even if carrots are past their best, they can be rejuvenated by adding a little baking soda to the cooking water. Adding the baking soda has a double effect: it helps the color and helps keep them crisp too.

White Cauliflower

Two tablespoons baking soda added to the cooking water when you are boiling a cauliflower will help keep the flower of the vegetable nice and white.

Crisp Corn

If you want to keep your corn on the cob crisp, why not try adding 2 tablespoons baking soda to the cooking water?

Soaking Beans

If you like to eat dried beans but want to soften them before cooking, you can help them along when soaking them overnight by adding 1 teaspoon baking soda to the water – with enough water to cover the beans fully.

Great Greens

To maintain the color of green vegetables, you can add ½ teaspoon baking soda to the cooking water. This works really well for green beans, broccoli and sprouts.

 CAUTION: Do not forget that you should never overcook your greens – if you do, most of the goodness ends up in the water.

First Class Cabbage

To reduce the cooking time of cabbage and to keep it tender, you just have to add 3 tablespoons baking soda to the cooking water. We all agree that there is nothing worse than overcooked cabbage!

Adding baking soda to your cabbage's cooking water can also help your family and friends avoid the ill effects of the vegetable's gasses after eating the meal. It must be much better for all concerned, I'm sure you agree!

 CAUTION: Although baking soda has a positive visual effect on vegetables, do not be tempted to add too much or get into a habit of using it all the time, as it can reportedly destroy the natural vitamins C and B1 in the veggies.

Speedy Tomato Sauce

If you are making your own tomato sauce or salsa, you can reduce the cooking time by adding some baking soda. Add 2 tablespoons baking soda for every 900 ml/1½ pts/scant 1 qt cooking water. This can reduce the cooking time by at least 10 minutes.

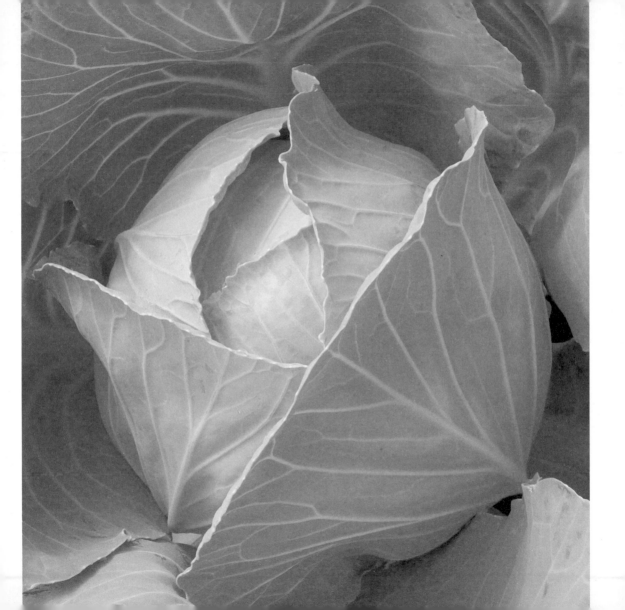

Sweeter Tomatoes

Adding baking soda to the water you are cooking your tomatoes in when preparing your salsa or tomato sauce can also help to neutralize the acid in the tomatoes.

Milder Veg

In order to remove the harsher and stronger flavor from some wild vegetables, add around 1 teaspoon baking soda per 1 l/1¾ pts/1 qt water when you boil your vegetables. The color of the vegetables also becomes brighter.

Clean Veg

You cannot be too careful when it comes to food handling and preparation. Wash your fruit and vegetables in cold water with 2–3 tablespoons baking soda added to it. This will help remove some of the impurities that our tap water leaves behind. For more thorough cleaning, the dirt in or on your fruit and vegetables will wash away so much more quickly and easily if you add 100 g/3½ oz/½ cup baking soda to the water.

To go further, if you want to be sure your shop-bought vegetables are chemical-free when you cook them, try washing them with 200 g/7 oz/1 cup baking soda added to a sinkful of fresh water. More and more of the ready-prepared vegetables and fruits look too good to be true – shiny fruit is often covered with edible wax, but baking soda will get rid of this for you.

Alternatively, you can dab a wet sponge or your vegetable brush into neat baking soda and use this to scrub your vegetables. The baking soda will remove the dirt, any wax and pesticides. Give everything a thorough rinsing before serving or cooking your vegetables.

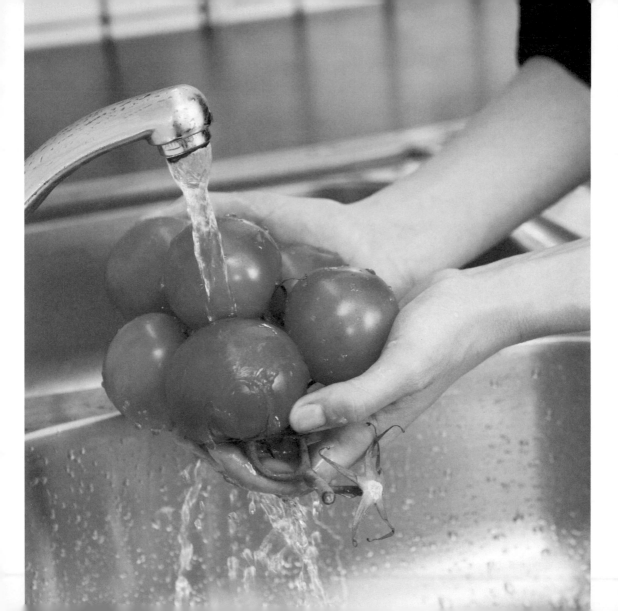

Other Uses

Baking Powder

Make your own baking powder by stirring and sifting together two parts cream of tartar to one part baking soda and one part cornstarch.

 CAUTION: Resist the urge to add more baking soda or baking powder than a recipe instructs, as this can cause the food to taste bitter and it can also cause it to rise too rapidly, causing the mixture to collapse. On the other hand, too little baking powder or baking soda leads to a tough and densely textured product.

Neutralize Acidity

There is plenty of citric acid in most fruits that can upset and inflame the stomach. You can neutralize the acid in coffee by adding 1 teaspoon baking soda to your cup or mug. Why not add it to the coffee pot when you make a fresh brew? Two or 3 teaspoons baking soda will be more than enough for everyone.

No More Beans Blues

You know how the saying goes: 'Beans, beans are good for your heart, the more you eat …' Well, to solve the excess gas problem, try adding 1 teaspoon baking soda to your baked beans when you are cooking them. All of the bean goodness is there without the unpleasant aftereffects!

Recipes

Baking soda has been used throughout the ages as a raising agent in baking. This is its principal use in food, either used directly or as part of baking powder. If there is already some sort of acid in the recipe, then baking soda can be used, as it will react with the acid once a liquid is added and then cause the carbon dioxide bubbles that enable the raising. Baking powder is used when there is no acid in the recipe.

Irish Soda Bread

Makes 1 loaf

400 g/14 oz/3¼ cups
    white all-purpose flour,
    plus 1 tbsp for dusting
1 tsp salt
2 tsp baking soda
15 g/½ oz/1 tbsp butter

50 g/2 oz/⅓ cup quick oats
1 tsp clear honey
300 ml/½ pt/1¼ cups buttermilk
2 tbsp milk

For a whole-wheat variation:

400 g/14 oz/3¼ cups
    whole-wheat flour,
    plus 1 tbsp for dusting
1 tbsp milk

1 Preheat the oven to 200°C/400°F/Gas Mark 6, 15 minutes before baking. Sift the flour, salt and baking soda into a large bowl. Rub in the butter until the mixture resembles fine breadcrumbs. Stir in the oatmeal and make a well in the centre.
2 Mix the honey, buttermilk and milk together and add to the dry ingredients. Mix to a soft dough.
3 Knead the dough on a lightly floured surface for 2–3 minutes until the dough is smooth. Shape into a 20.5 cm/8 inch round and place on an oiled baking sheet.
4 Thickly dust the top of the bread with flour. Using a sharp knife, cut a deep cross on top, going about halfway through the loaf.
5 Bake in the preheated oven on the middle shelf for 30–35 minutes until the bread is slightly risen, golden and sounds hollow when tapped underneath. Cool on a wire rack. Eat on the day of making.
6 For a whole-wheat soda bread, use all the whole wheat flour instead of the white flour and add an extra tablespoon of milk when mixing together. Dust the top with whole wheat flour and bake.

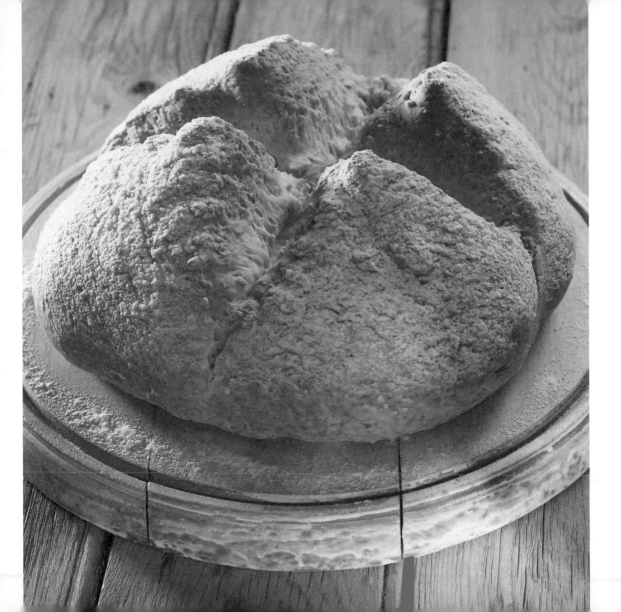

Fruity Apple Teabread

Cuts into 12 slices

125 g/4 oz/½ cup butter

125 g/4 oz/½ cup soft light
brown sugar

275 g/10 oz/2 cups
golden raisins

150 ml/¼ pint/⅔ cup apple juice

1 apple, peeled, cored
and chopped

2 eggs, beaten

275 g/10 oz/2¼ cups
all-purpose flour

½ tsp ground cinnamon

½ tsp ground ginger

2 tsp baking soda

butter curls, to serve

To decorate:

1 apple, cored and sliced

1 tsp lemon juice

1 tbsp corn syrup, warmed

1 Preheat the oven to 180°C/350°F/Gas Mark 4. Oil and line the base of a 900 g/2 lb loaf pan with nonstick baking paper.

2 Put the butter, sugar, golden raisins and apple juice in a small saucepan. Heat gently, stirring occasionally, until the butter has melted. Tip into a bowl and leave to cool.

3 Stir in the chopped apple and beaten eggs. Sift in the flour, spices and baking soda and stir together. Spoon into the prepared loaf pan and smooth the top level with the back of a spoon.

4 Toss the apple slices in lemon juice and arrange on top. Bake in the preheated oven for 50 minutes. Cover with foil to prevent the top from browning too much.

5 Bake for 30–35 minutes until a skewer inserted into the centre comes out clean. Leave in the tin for 10 minutes before turning out to cool on to a wire rack.

6 Brush the top with syrup and leave to cool. Remove the lining paper, cut into thick slices and serve with curls of butter.

Carrot Cake

Cuts into 8 slices

200 g/7 oz/1⅓ cups
   all-purpose flour
½ tsp ground cinnamon
½ tsp freshly grated nutmeg
1 tsp baking powder
1 tsp baking soda
150 g/5 oz/⅔ cup dark
   brown sugar

200 ml/7 fl oz/¾ cup
   vegetable oil
3 eggs
225 g/8 oz/1¼ cups carrots,
   peeled and roughly grated
50 g/2 oz/½ cup
   chopped walnuts

For the icing:

175 g/6 oz/¾ cup cream cheese
finely grated zest of 1 orange
1 tbsp orange juice
1 tsp vanilla extract
125 g/4 oz/1 cup
   confectioners' sugar

1 Preheat the oven to 150°C/300°F/Gas Mark 2, 10 minutes before baking. Lightly oil and line the base of a 15 cm/6 inch deep square cake pan with nonstick baking paper.

2 Sift the flour, spices, baking powder and baking soda together into a large bowl. Stir in the dark brown sugar and mix together.

3 Lightly whisk the oil and eggs together, then gradually stir into the flour and sugar mixture. Stir well. Add the carrots and walnuts. Mix thoroughly, then pour into the prepared cake tin. Bake in the preheated oven for 1¼ hours, or until light and springy to the touch and a skewer inserted into the centre of the cake comes out clean.

4 Remove from the oven and allow to cool in the pan for 5 minutes before turning out on to a wire rack. Reserve until cold.

5 To make the icing, beat together the cream cheese, orange zest and juice and vanilla extract. Sift in the confectioners' sugar and stir. When the cake is cold, discard the lining paper, spread the cream cheese icing over the top and serve cut into squares.

Easy Chocolate Cake

Serves 8–10

75 g/3 oz dark chocolate,
  broken into squares
200 ml/7 fl oz/¾ cup milk
250 g/9 oz/1¼ cups dark
  brown sugar
75 g/3 oz/⅓ cup (6 tbsp) butter,
  softened

2 medium/large eggs, beaten
150 g/5 oz/1 heaped cup
  all-purpose flour
½ tsp vanilla extract
1 tsp baking soda
25 g/1 oz/¼ cup unsweetened
  cocoa powder

For the topping and filling:

125 g/4 oz/½ cup (1 stick)
  unsalted butter
225 g/8 oz/2¼ cups
  confectioners' sugar, sifted
8 large fresh strawberries, halved
tiny mint sprigs, to decorate

1 Preheat the oven to 180°C/350°F/Gas Mark 4. Grease two 20.5 cm/8 inch round layer-cake pans and line the bases with nonstick baking paper.

2 Place the chocolate, milk and 75 g/3 oz/⅓ cup of the sugar in a heavy-based saucepan. Heat gently until the mixture has melted, then set aside to cool.

3 Place the butter and remaining sugar in a large bowl and whisk with an electric mixer until light and fluffy. Gradually whisk in the eggs, adding 1 teaspoon flour with each addition.

4 Stir in the cooled melted chocolate mixture along with the vanilla extract. Sift in the flour, baking soda and cocoa powder, then fold into the mixture until smooth.

5 Spoon the batter into the pans and smooth level. Bake for about 30 minutes until a skewer inserted into the centre comes out clean. Turn out to cool on a wire rack.

6 To decorate, beat the butter with the confectioners' sugar and 1 tablespoon warm water until light and fluffy, then place half in a piping bag fitted with a star nozzle.

7 Spread half the buttercream over one sponge layer and scatter half the strawberries over it. Top with the other cake and spread the remaining buttercream over the top. Pipe a border of stars around the edge. Decorate with the remaining strawberries and mint sprigs.

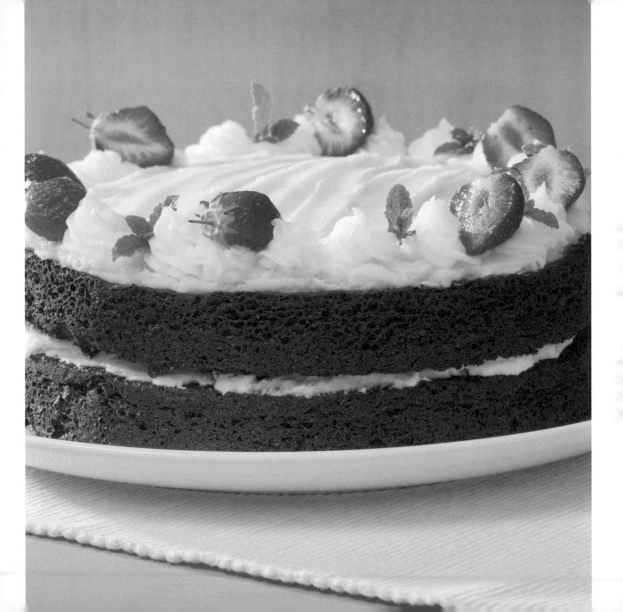

Gingerbread Cookies

**Makes 20 large or
28 small cookies**

225 g/8 oz/1¾ cups all-purpose
 flour, plus extra for dusting
½ tsp ground ginger
½ tsp mixed spice

½ tsp baking soda
75 g/3 oz/⅓ cup (6 tbsp) butter
2 tbsp corn syrup
1 tbsp molasses
75 g/3 oz/⅓ cup soft dark
 brown sugar

50 g/2 oz/scant ½ cup royal
 icing sugar or confectioners'
 sugar, to decorate

1 Preheat the oven to 180°C/350°F/Gas Mark 4 and grease two baking sheets. Sift the
 flour, spices and baking soda into a bowl.

2 Place the butter, syrup, molasses and sugar in a heavy-based pan with 1 tablespoon
 water and heat gently until every grain of sugar has dissolved and the butter has melted.
 Cool for 5 minutes, then pour the melted mixture into the dry ingredients and mix to a
 soft dough.

3 Leave the dough, covered, for 30 minutes. Roll out the dough on a lightly floured surface
 to a 3 mm/⅛ inch thickness and cut out fancy shapes. Gather up the trimmings and re-roll
 the dough, cutting out more shapes. Place on the baking sheets using a spatula and bake
 for about 10 minutes until golden and firm. Be careful not to overcook, as the cookies will
 brown quickly.

4 Decorate the cookies by mixing the royal icing sugar or confectioners' sugar with enough
 water to make a piping consistency. Place the icing in a small paper piping bag with the
 end snipped away and pipe faces and decorations on to the biscuits.

Oatmeal Raisin Cookies

Makes 24

175 g/6 oz/1½ cups
all-purpose flour
150 g/5 oz/2 cups rolled oats
1 tsp ground ginger

½ tsp baking powder
½ tsp baking soda
125 g/4 oz/⅔ cup
turbinado sugar
50 g/2 oz/⅓ cup raisins

1 large egg, lightly beaten
150 ml/¼ pint/⅔ cup vegetable
or sunflower/corn oil
4 tbsp milk

1 Preheat the oven to 200°C/400°F/Gas Mark 6, 15 minutes before baking. Lightly oil a baking sheet.
2 Mix together the flour, oats, ground ginger, baking powder, baking soda, sugar and the raisins in a large bowl.
3 In another bowl, mix the egg, oil and milk together. Make a well in the centre of the dry ingredients and pour in the egg mixture.
4 Mix the mixture together well with either a fork or a wooden spoon to make a soft but not sticky dough.
5 Place spoonfuls of the dough well apart on the oiled baking sheet and flatten the tops down slightly with the tines of a fork.
6 Transfer the biscuits to the preheated oven and bake for 10–12 minutes until golden.
7 Remove from the oven, leave to cool for 2–3 minutes, then transfer the biscuits to a wire rack to cool. Serve when cold or otherwise store in an airtight container.

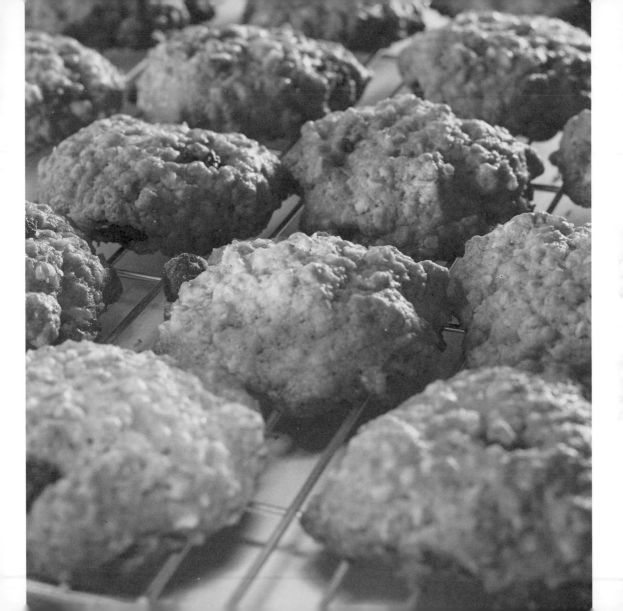

Further Reading

Briggs, M., *Bicarbonate of Soda: A Very Versatile Natural Substance*, Black and White Publishing, 2007

Briggs, M., *Green Cleaning: Natural Hints and Tips*, Abbeydale Press, 2008

Briggs, M., *Vinegar – 1001 Practical Uses*, Abbeydale Press, 2006

Constantino, M., *Household Hints*, Flame Tree, 2009

Fraser, R., *Neal's Yard Remedies Recipes for Natural Beauty*, Haldane Mason Ltd, 2007

Grace, J. L., *Imperfectly Natural Home: The Organic Bible*, Orion, 2008

Hamilton, A., *The Self Sufficient-ish Bible*, Hodder & Stoughton, 2009

Harrison, J., *Low-Cost Living: Live better, spend less*, Right Way, 2009

Lansky, V., *Baking Soda: Over 500 Fabulous, Fun, and Frugal Uses You've Probably Never Thought of*, Book Peddlers, 2008

Logan, K.N., *Clean House, Clean Planet: Clean Your House for Pennies a Day, the Safe, Nontoxic Way*, Simon & Schuster, 1997

Martin, A., *Natural Stain Remover: Clean Your Home Without Harmful Chemicals*, Apple Press, 2003

Peacock, D., *Good Home Cooking: Make it, Don't Buy It! Real Food at Home – Mostly at Less Than a Pound a Head*, Spring Hill 2009

Peacock, P., *Grandma's Ways for Modern Days: Relearning Traditional Self-sufficiency – Gardening, Cooking and Household Management*, Spring Hill, 2009

Reader's Digest, *Extraordinary Uses For Ordinary Things: 2,209 Ways to Save Money and Time*, Reader's Digest, 2008

Reader's Digest, *1001 Home Remedies: Trustworthy Treatments for Everyday Health Problems*, Reader's Digest, 2005

Strawbridge, D., & Strawbridge, J., *Practical Self Sufficiency: The Complete Guide to Sustainable Living*, Dorling Kindersley, 2010

Websites

www.armhammer.com
The official website for the Arm & Hammer baking soda company. It offers practical uses for baking soda, including a section on projects for kids.

www.babycentre.co.uk
A website that offers plenty of advice about caring for babies from pregnancy to preschool.

www.bbc.co.uk/food/campaigns/get-baking
The BBC encourages readers online to 'get baking' by offering various recipes – many of which contain baking soda.

www.channel4.com/food/recipes/baking
A website that offers many baking ideas, including many recipes that involve baking soda.

www.doityourself.com
A website that offers various DIY tips and projects.

www.enjo.org.uk
A website that offers chemical-free, environmentally friendly cleaning products for all areas of the home.

www.hygieneexpert.co.uk
A website that offers hygiene advice and information for humans as well as pets.

www.gardenersworld.com
A website with tips and guides for gardeners of any experience level.

www.grist.org
An environmentally conscious news site that gives tips on DIY projects and green living.

www.home-remedies-for-you.com
A website that offers treatments for a plethora of ailments using common household products, including good old baking soda.

www.treehugger.com
A website that focuses entirely on green living. It contains news about the latest environmentally friendly technology as well as advice on how to make a positive environmental impact.

www.ultimatehandyman.co.uk
A website that offers advice on DIY home improvement and gives instructions on undertaking many household DIY projects.

www.wackyuses.com
A website that offers unusual but helpful uses for common household products.

Picture Credits

The following images are © **Flame Tree Publishing Ltd**: 5b, 211, 215, 236, 239–249. All other images are courtesy of **Shutterstock** and © the following photographers: 1 & 207, 4t & 40 & 47, 227 Monkey Business Images; 3 & 139, 138 auremar; 4c & 101 Anthony Harris; 4b & 157 Karen H. Ilgan; 5t & 181 Gemenacom; 5c & 205 HP_photo; 6 & 120 & 129, 44 Diego Cervo; 7 Andre Klaassen; 8 Picsfive; 9, 12 matka_Wariatka; 10 Jonathan Vasata; 11 & 137 Kurhan; 14 & 23, 143 Julija Sapic; 15 oleksa; 16 Victoria Alexandrova; 17 Photoroller; 19 Irina Fischer; 21 Tom Baker; 22 & 237 artproem; 24 Daniel Krylov; 25 James M Phelps Jr; 27 Ragne Kabanova; 29 jokerpro; 31 Anne Kitzman; 33 Tomasz Trojanowski; 35 Paul Cowan; 37 Muriel Lasure; 39 Cheryl Casey; 41 yampi; 42, 118 digieye; 43 Brian A Jackson; 45 Crystal Kirk; 46 Tiplyashin Anatoly; 48 Alistair Scott; 49 Baloncici; 50 Freerk Brouwer; 51 Yellowj; 52 Paul Maguire; 53 Daniel Goodings; 54 & 57, 58 Konovalikov Andrey; 55 Gorin; 56 aceshot1; 59 terekhov igor; 60 Margo Harrison; 61 michaeljung; 62 Kimberly Hall; 63, 103 Peter Gudella; 64, 123 jkitan; 65 Joe Belanger; 67, 177 Jaimie Duplass; 68 Freddy Eliasson; 69 Shane White; 71 Olga Chernetskaya; 72 Darren A Hubley; 73 Maria Dryfhout; 75 Leifstiller; 76 Alkristeena; 77 PAUL ATKINSON; 79 & 159 Zholobov Vadim; 80 & 160 & 165, 145 Elena Elisseeva; 81 Lisa Turay; 83 ushama; 85 Maridav; 87 photogl; 88 & 95 Carrieanne Larmore; 89 Vuk Nenezic; 90 Baevskiy Dmitry; 91 & 251 Michelle D Milliman; 92 iofoto; 93 Slasha; 96 Thomas Skjæveland; 97 Sarah Salmela; 98 ZTS; 100 pixelman; 105, 188 teekaygee; 107 Eric Gevaert; 109 Petro Feketa; 111 Agb; 113 Jean Valley; 115 Mirco Vacca; 116 Stephen VanHorn; 117 Dmitriy Yakovlev; 121 rebvt; 122 Piotr Marcinski; 125 Rene Jansa; 126 Danijel Micka; 127 Skazka Grez; 131 Anthony Berenyi; 132 Alexey Stiop; 133 Netfalls; 134 imageshunter; 135 kristian sekulic; 136 Camilo Torres; 140 paul prescott; 141 StockLite; 142 sevenke; 146 & 155 Vasina Natalia; 147 elaine hudson; 148 charles taylor; 149 Wojciech Zbieg; 150 Gaby Kooijman; 151 Artur Bogacki; 152 Kristy Pargeter; 153 Zsolt Nyulaszi; 154r James R T Bossert; 154l Kafer photo; 158, 202 & 213 Ieva Geneciviene; 161 Edw; 162 gsplanet; 163 Miodrag Gajic; 167 Tobik; 168 efirm; 170 & 173 Vasily Mulyukin; 171 Scott L. Williams; 172 Colleen Farrell; 174 david n madden; 175 kreego; 176 Nancy Kennedy; 179 Stuart Monk; 180 dendong; 182, 183 Alena Brozova; 185 Pakhnyushcha; 186 Johanna Goodyear; 187 Andrey Pavlov; 189 Vaclav Volrab; 190 Ramona Heim; 191 Mona Makela; 192 Christina Richards; 193 Losevsky Pavel; 194 & 199 Dmitry Naumov; 195 SNEHIT; 197 Jason Stitt; 198 yazan masa; 200 Kruchankova Maya; 203 Aleksandar-Pal Sakala; 204 Alex Staroseltsev; 209 Robert Anthony; 212 travis manley; 214 bierchen; 216 Roxana Bashyrova; 217 Whitechild; 218 holbox; 219 Noam Armonn; 220 Magdalena Kucova; 222 & 233 Tyler Olson; 223 Ermes; 224 Jacek Chabraszewski; 225 David P. Smith; 228 Richard Griffin; 229 Rey Kamensky; 231 Denis and Yulia Pogostins; 235 Elke Dennis.

Index

index